S0-AAC-412

A Dress
for Mona

A Dress for Mona

A play by Mark Perry

5TH EPOCH PRESS
www.adressformona.org

Fifth Epoch Press (an imprint of Discover Writing Press)
PO Box 264
Shoreham, VT 05770
1-800-613-8055
fax # 802-897-2084
www.discoverwriting.com

Anyone wishing to produce this play
Contact Discover Writing Company 1-800-613-8055
for royalty rates and discounts on bulk purchases.
No performance may be given without permission.

Copyright © 2002 by Mark E. Perry
ISBN # 1-931492-02-6
Library of Congress 2002090786

All rights reserved. No part of this work may be reproduced or transmitted in any form or by any means, electronic or mechanical, including photocopying and recording, or by any information storage or retrieval system, except as may be expressly permitted by the 1976 Copyright Act or in writing by the publisher, or for limited use in the classroom.

02 03 04 05 06 07   10 9 8 7 6 5 4 3 2 1

TO MONA,

TO YADU'LLAH,

TO THOSE WHO PRECEDED THEM,

TO THOSE WHO HAVE FOLLOWED

On the day you put me in the grave
Remember my confusion
Remember all the fears I felt
Fill the little room
At the bottom of the tomb
With your light
I want to be part of your harvest of roses
I want to walk into your hall
Like an ant coming to see Solomon
All I want is your presence
And this silence
You finish this

RUMI

Table of Contents

ACT I

ACT II

SUPPLEMENTARY MATERIALS

Acknowledgments

I am indebted to Olya Roohizadegan, whose book, *Olya's Story* (Oxford: Oneworld Publications, 1993), is the primary source of historical information available on the life of Mona Mahmudnizhad. Special thanks go to Alan MacVey, Art Borreca, Dare Clubb, Naomi Iizuka, Erik Ehn, Kristen Gandrow, Willie Barbour, Tressa and Edward Clifton, the members and many guests of the Iowa Playwrights Workshop and the many others in Iowa, Oregon and Florida who have helped in the process of developing the script. Special thanks also to Lynne Yancy and the Bahá'í Literature Review Office for their recommendations, to Amrollah Hemmat for his wisdom, to Monír R., Parvíz M., Saíd A. and the other friends in Iran for their assistance. My deep gratitude goes out to Phyllis Ring, who had a good word at the very beginning, to Barry Lane for his support throughout, and, finally, to Azadeh, the little-suspected miracle.

Introduction

On the 18th of June, 1983 in Shíráz, Iran, ten women were executed by hanging for their unwillingness to renounce their Bahá'í belief in the face of the Islamic fundamentalism that had recently overtaken their country. This act was particularly disturbing since usually only Bahá'í men were targeted for execution. The incident brought outcries from the world community appealing to the Iranian government to implement basic human rights for the Bahá'ís. This international pressure had its effect in that recent years have witnessed fewer executions, but Bahá'ís are still denied basic rights of education, employment, assembly and legal protection. The Bahá'í Faith is a religion native to Iran and is considered apostasy by the religious leaders of Shí'ih Islam. Since the religion began in 1844, over 20,000 of its adherents have been martyred. Of the ten women executed in 1983, the youngest was 16 years old. Her name was Mona Mahmúdni<u>zh</u>ád.*

Stories of saints are plentiful. Compelling and engaging plays about them are not. The lives of saints don't seem to be the stuff of which drama is made. Drama is about moral ambiguity, tragic flaws and comic vices. We want to see someone like us up on the stage, or better yet, someone worse off than us — someone who kills his father and sleeps with his mother! Oddly, we attain catharsis by watching some straw man, on whom we heap our repressed anxieties and desires, as he is beat about on stage by an ironic and moralizing Fate. (This may account as well for our laughter at comedy as our horror at tragedy.) On the other hand, the

---

* There is some confusion among sources about Mona's age. Some say she was 16, some say 17, and some say 18. According to her sister, Taránih, she was born 19 Shahrivar 1345 (10 September 1966 C.E.), which would make her 16 years 9 months and 8 days when she was executed. In the play, therefore, Mona is 16.

steady virtue of the saints, admirable though it may be, can hardly hold our attention, much less compete with the volatility of vice in dispensing pleasure. Perhaps we best leave the subject of sainthood to the stained-glass renderings of the Cathedral. There they remain, in their two-dimensional splendor, floating up above us — stars in the sky — to be turned to in time of need, beseeched for a favor, for a guiding light.

Such a celestial entity to me was Mona. As a young Bahá'í, I remember hearing the story, even in the national media, of the young exemplar of fortitude in the face of horrid abusiveness. In the mid-1980's, a Canadian musician named Doug Cameron released the song, "Mona with the Children," with an accompanying video that was effective in spreading the story. As songs usually do, it captured the emotion of the story, but not the drama. And there was drama lurking there. The story felt like it could be told through theatre, except that Mona seemed super-human. How do we relate to someone like that?

I had the privilege in 1994 of hearing Olya Roohizadegan, one of Mona's fellow prisoners, speak. She had been released some months before the ten women were executed. One of the key points of her talk, and one that impressed me considerably, was the humanity of these people. Mona, this great figure, was really a *girl* — a girl of sixteen, seventeen, who was remarkable in many ways, but who still had some of the same cares and concerns as so many others her age. She told the story of a dream Mona had before going into prison, a dream that would have a profound effect on her life. It was the dream of three dresses. Without going into the detail of the dream (since it provides a sort of backbone for the play), I can say that Mona's response in that dream was something I could understand, something I could relate to. I went home and wrote it down. I rarely do things like that.

Almost five years later, in contemplating what story I wanted to devote a summer to fashioning, I thought of Mona and her dream of three dresses. It was an "in," a place to begin. To me, her choice in the dream indicated a journey. It indicated Mona did not end where she began. By the time she was martyred, she had traversed vast spiritual territory. Now was it possible for us to benefit from her transformation in that special way theatre sometimes allows? I was willing to invest some time. The play eventually took a lot longer than a summer to come to fruition, but that was okay. The story has a power that has continued to sustain me, inspiring me to return to it.

A Dress for Mona is a play based on Mona's life, but it's not intended as a document of history. It is a work of fiction and liberties have been taken with historical fact in service of — what is hoped to be — dramatic truth. One of the tools in the hand of the playwright when approaching history is the conflation of time and place. Basically, this means you combine significant events that happened over a long time period and in many locales in order to concentrate sprawling Life into a relatively few, easy-to-connect scenes. For example: in actuality, there were almost three years from the time of the destruction of the House of the Báb to the day of Mona's arrest; in the play, it seems to happen within 24 hours.

Another tool in the hand of the playwright when approaching history is the choice of factual or fictional characters. Mona, Yadu'lláh and Farkhundih Mahmúdnizhád are all real, and I have tried to recreate some of the essentials of their relationships. The biggest modification I have made involves Mona's mother, Farkhundih. Although she was the only one of the three to survive, she, like the others, spent many difficult months in prison suffering for her belief. Another character based on an actual person is Fakhrí (the head prisoner at Sepah prison). The Religious Magistrate, Áyatu'lláh Qazá'í, was the individual who gave the order for the women to be put to death. His characterization here, however, is fictional. The role of Áqá Husayní conflates a couple of clerical figures, and then some. Mr. Alizadeh, Mrs. Khudayar, Farah, and Aram are entirely made up, as are most of the minor parts.

Probably the greatest departure the character Mona takes from the historical Mona comes in those moments of questioning, doubting and fear that erupt in the prison scenes. From all indications, Mona showed indomitable faith and courage in prison. The problem with presenting this dramatically is twofold: first, as an audience, we have a hard time connecting with a flat-out saint, and we will distance ourselves from one who appears to be a fanatic; second, and more importantly, the truth is Mona had to make a spiritual journey at some point. Spiritual journeys imply questioning. They imply going from weakness to strength, doubt to certainty, etc. This play is an attempt at dramatizing Mona's, and every person's, journey. The Rumi poem offered as an epigraph ("*remember my confusion . . . all the fears I felt*") is offered simultaneously as an apology and a justification for this decision.

A Dress for Mona was first performed at the University of Iowa as a Gallery Production in March 2001. The play was directed by Mark Perry. The cast and crew of the play included:

Mona .... *Terra Gillespie*

Father .... *Kehry Lane*

Mother / Girl (in English class) .... *Briana Sprecher*

Young Man – Aram – Religious Magistrate .... *Aaron Galbraith*

Mr. Alizadeh .... *Tim Budd*

Aqa Husayni .... *Ari Herbstmann*

Farah / Zahra / Guard .... *Kristen Gast*

Mrs. Khudayar / School Secretary /
Head Prisoner .... *Cristela Carrizales*

Dramaturg .... *Azadeh Rohanian*

Stage and Lighting Design .... *Rob Koop*

Stage Manager .... *Gretchen Welker*

Assistant Stage Manager .... *Brian Finley*

Costume Design .... *Tallie Nelson*

Light Board Operator .... *Liga Rostocks*

Sound Board Operator .... *Chris Jones*

Setting & Cast of Characters

Shiraz, Iran. The early years of the Islamic Revolution (c. 1979–1983 C.E.)

Character		Approximate Pronunciation
MONA (MAHMÚDNIZHÁD)	*16; friendly and bright, not yet a saint*	mah-MOOD-ne-ZHAD
FATHER (YADU'LLÁH MAHMÚDNIZHÁD)	*Middle-aged; devout, with youthful exuberance*	YA-do-LA
MOTHER (FÁRKHUNDIH MAHMÚDNIZHÁD)	*Middle-aged; anxious, strong-willed*	FAR-kon-DEH
ÁRÁM (HUSAYNÍ)*	*16; self-assured, a bit peculiar, in love with Mona*	ar-AHM ho-SAY-nee
YOUNG MAN *	*Ageless; Mona's guide and Animus*	
RELIGIOUS MAGISTRATE (ÁYATU'LLÁH QAZÁ'Í)*	*Older; powerful, dominating, fanatical*	AH-ya-TO-la ga-ZA-ee
MR. ALÍZÁDEH	*Middle-aged; charismatic, Mona's teacher*	a-LEE-za-DEH

*Characters to be portrayed by a single actor.

ÁQÁ HUSAYNÍ	*Middle-aged; a religious cleric, adamant*	AH-ga ho-SAY-nee
FARAH (JA'FARÍ)	*16; bold and worldly, Mona's friend*	FA-rah ja-FAR-ee
MRS. KHUDÁYÁR	*Middle-aged; a snooping neighbor*	KO-da-YAR
HEAD PRISONER (FAKHRÍ)	*a political prisoner, shrewd*	FAK-ree
ZAHRÁ	*a drug addict in withdrawal, young*	ZAH-ra
SCHOOL SECRETARY	*a woman longing for the days of the Sháh*	
GUARD	*a man not yet grown into his gun*	
GIRL (IN MR. ALIZADEH'S CLASS)	*a blabbermouth on a hair trigger*	

Minimum cast requirements: 4 female; 4 male

(See *Notes from First Production*, p. 128)

A DRESS FOR MONA

ACT I

Scene 1 – Mona's Dream

Darkness. The sound of water. A large, empty picture frame is illuminated center stage. MONA, *a young woman in her teens, enters from the back of the auditorium, and walks to the frame. She looks into it as if it was a mirror, assessing her looks.*

MONA: Mmm.

Mona's FATHER *is revealed downstage. He very precisely slices an orange with a knife. He speaks to Mona in Persian.*

FATHER: Ye chíz míkhám behet begam.
(Translated: I want to tell you something.)

A pounding. Mona's MOTHER *is revealed upstage, sitting on the floor, which she pounds with her fist.*

MOTHER: Báyad bídárshí.
(Translated: You have to wake up.)

FATHER: Valí báyad sabr koní.
(Translated: But you have to wait.)

MOTHER: Dokhtar-am, pásho!
(Translated: My daughter, get up!)

See *Persian Pronunciation Guide* (p. 127) for readings and productions.

Mona's teacher, MR. ALIZADEH, *enters from house left. He carries a carpet.*

MR. ALIZADEH: Ghálí míkháhí? To ín ghálí-ro lázem dárí.
  (Translated: Do you want a carpet? You need this carpet.)

Mona's friend, FARAH, *is revealed upstage. She has a large black cloth that she throws off, hide and seek style.*

FARAH: Man ínjám! *(She throws the cloth back over her head.)* Kojá raftam?
  (Translated: Here I am! Where'd I go?)

MR. ALIZADEH: To ín ghálí-ro lázem dárí!
  (Translated: You need this carpet.)

A knocking comes from stage left. The mother picks up a nearby phone.

MOTHER: Pásho.
  (Translated: Get up.)

Mona's neighbor, MRS. KHUDAYAR, *peeks in.*

MRS. KHUDAYAR: Bad moghast?
  (Translated: Is this a bad time?)

MR. ALIZADEH *(pulling out a book)*: Ye ketáb?
  (Translated: A book?)

FARAH: Man ínjám!
  (Translated: Here I am!)

They all begin to speak their phrases. Adding to the cacophony is an Islamic call to prayer that comes over a loudspeaker.

MONA: Okay, okay, okay! That's enough!

Blackout and sound-out. Silence.

MONA (*in darkness*): Wait. Wait. That's not what I want. (*A beat.*) Hey. Help me. Help me.

FATHER: Would you like me to turn the light off for you?

MONA (*in darkness*): What? No. Not yet.

> MONA *strikes a match.* VOICES *whisper:* "Here", "this way", "I've got it", "Who's there?" *etc., or appropriate lines from the rest of the play.* MONA *begins to walk one way. A* SMILING FACE *appears next to the match and blows it out.*

MONA: Hey!

> *No response.* MONA *lights another match and looks around. More whispering. An* ANGRY FACE *appears and blows the match out.*

MONA: I. Need. Light.

> *A hush. An unlit candle is briefly illuminated.*

MONA: Thank you.

> MONA *walks to it, strikes another match and lights the candle. She lifts the candle and takes it back to place it before the picture frame. Behind the frame, a* ROBED FIGURE *is illuminated.*

A VOICE: A gift.

TWO FOICES: From.

ALL: God.

> *Silence. The* ROBED FIGURE *gestures right. A red dress is revealed. Whispers.* MONA *takes the dress and holds it up to herself. There is a sudden reveal of a* GIRL *being hanged.*

MONA: No!

The image is gone as quickly as it came. The ROBED FIGURE *gestures left. A black dress is revealed. Whispers.* MONA *again holds the dress up to herself. Reveal of a scene with a* GIRL *moaning, as if starving.*

MONA: No! No! I don't want that either.

The image is gone. The ROBED FIGURE *comes forward and reveals a blue dress. Whispers.* MONA *slowly takes it and holds it up to herself. The* ROBED FIGURE *whispers in* MONA's *ear. The light around her grows brighter. Another hush falls.*

MONA: Yes. This is the dress I choose.

The ROBED FIGURE *removes his hood, unveiling a handsome* YOUNG MAN. MONA *is captivated. As he speaks he eventually moves back behind the frame.*

MONA: Who are you?

YOUNG MAN: Look for me.

MONA: What?

YOUNG MAN: I am there when you look for me.

MONA: When I . . . ? What do you . . . ?

YOUNG MAN: In the face of others—

MONA: What do you mean?

YOUNG MAN: Look for me.

MONA: I don't know what you mean.

YOUNG MAN: Look for me.

MONA: Who are you?

Mona's MOTHER's *voice is heard, calling to her. This time from the waking world.*

MOTHER (*off*): Mona!

YOUNG MAN (*behind the frame*): I am . . .

MOTHER: Mona, my dear, wake up. You've left the light on.

The YOUNG MAN *pulls the hood back over his head and exits into the dark with the dress as the scene shifts to Mona's room.*

MONA: Mother. I'm awake.

MONA *puts out the candle.*

Scene 2 – A Street in Shiraz, Iran

MONA *looks stunned, as the remnants of her dream are swept off-stage.*

MONA: Shopping. (*Pause.*) I want to go shopping. (*Pause.*) Farah. Let's go shopping.

FARAH: You know I'm game.

Mona's friend, FARAH, *emerges and joins* MONA. *They walk.*

FARAH: Okay, so he's acting like he is in control, like he's the man. And he works up his mouth like he just bit into a sour lime like I'm going to kiss that? Excuse me, little boy, I said. I said, two things you need to know. One, don't ever do your lips like that again. Two, you get nothing, nothing, unless you got a ring for this finger. This is what I said. I said it just like this. You want the control you get from Islam, but you like the freedom of the West too. But I'll tell you one thing. Give me a veil or give me a mini-skirt. But keep your controlling hands off Farah unless you're ready to buy the whole package.

MONA: Sounds like shopping.

FARAH: Exactly, but this item is not on sale. He wants me, he pays full price. So where are we going?

MONA: Huh?

FARAH: Hello, I'm talking to you!

MONA: Sorry, Farah, I'm just somewhere else. . .

FARAH: Dreaming again?

MONA: Mmm.

FARAH: Right, but I don't get it exactly. I mean what was the word you used?

MONA: Service.

FARAH: Right. You have to live a life of service, but what does that mean?

MONA: It seemed very clear in the dream.

FARAH: It seems really vague. Maybe you can ask God to give you the dream again and this time He could go into some more detail.

MONA: I don't think I need it.

FARAH: Who are you going to serve? I mean if you had money, you might be able to build people houses and give them food and clothing, but you don't.

MONA: No.

FARAH: So how then?

MONA: I don't know.

FARAH: But you think shopping is the first step.

MONA: Yes.

FARAH: I like the way this girl thinks.

MONA: Farah, I want my life to mean something. I don't want one where I just look after myself, where it's just me I'm worried about.

FARAH: Well, personally, I don't mind looking after myself, but then I have no crisis of conscience at the moment.

MONA: For the moment.

FARAH: You're sixteen years old. You haven't finished school. The world is full of war, death and turmoil, unspeakable poverty that the most powerful leaders of the world can't fix . . . What do you think you're going to do about it?

MONA: I don't know yet!

FARAH: What are you supposed to buy?

MONA: That's a surprise.

FARAH: I got it! Maybe you're supposed to get married.

MONA *looks at* FARAH *in disbelief.*

FARAH: No, listen! Maybe it was a wedding dress.

MONA: A blue wedding dress?

FARAH: Your favorite color, besides white is going out, everyone knows that.

MONA: I really doubt it.

FARAH: Was there a guy in this dream? Maybe you saw your future husband.

MONA: There was.

FARAH: Yeah? A guy? What'd he look like?

MONA: Well . . .

FARAH: Did you recognize him?

MONA: No. And I don't think . . . Farah, now you got me completely off track. Wait. Where are we?

FARAH: You're the one who led us here. I thought you knew where you were going.

MONA: Oh, no.

FARAH: Great, now we're lost.

MONA: Hold on a second. You think this dream is about marriage.

FARAH: I'm just saying, there's a dress, a man and a service.

MONA: Not a service!

FARAH: How else do women serve in Iran? They keep the fire going, the rice cooking and the babies coming.

MONA: You know where we are? This is the way to the house of the Báb. We're right around the corner.

FARAH: House of the what?

MONA: It's a . . . Anyway, I've come here since I was small. I must have just unconsciously walked this way.

FARAH: My guess is if we take this alley up here, we'll get back on track.

MONA: Farah, hold on. I think I need to stop by this house here.

FARAH: Why?

MONA: Can you wait for me?

FARAH: How long?

MONA: Not long.

FARAH: Then why can't I come?

MONA: It's religious . . .

FARAH: I know religion.

MONA: You know about my religion.

FARAH: I know something.

MONA: You may be safer if you're ignorant.

FARAH: That's what all religions say.

MONA: Fine. It's a holy place.

FARAH: Okay, and why are we going there?

MONA: You can come if you want, I just thought you might not want to.

FARAH: I might not. I have problems enough in my life without being seen at one of your holy places.

MONA: That's fine, Farah. Stay here.

FARAH: But then I might want to come.

MONA: Farah.

FARAH: Maybe if you tell me why you're going and stop being so elusive.

MONA: This dream is very important. Now that I'm here, I'm thinking I should go and pray for an answer. Or some guidance for what it might mean. Who knows? By the time I come out, the answer may be staring me in the face.

FARAH: Fine.

MONA: Okay?

> MONA *approaches the house and immediately changes her aspect, becoming reverent. Silence. She speaks in a hushed tone.*

MONA: This is it.

FARAH: Oh.

MONA: You can see where the guards tried to tear it down.

FARAH: Why did they stop?

MONA: A wall fell on one of them.

FARAH: Kill him?

MONA: Mm-hmm.

FARAH: Wow. But wait, hasn't this been confiscated?

MONA: This house doesn't belong to people who put up signs. It belongs to God. (*Slipping off her shoes at the gate.*) Anyway, they still let us come and go. Are you coming in?

FARAH: I don't know if I should. How long are you going to be?

MONA: Five minutes. Ten minutes.

FARAH: So what is this place again?

MONA: This is where my faith began.

FARAH: Oh.

MONA: A hundred and thirty five years ago.

FARAH: Oh. It's nice.

MONA: Are you coming in? Because if you stay out here, they'll probably see you and ask you who you are and what you're doing here.

FARAH: Who?

MONA: The mullas in the mosque across the street.

FARAH: What?!

MONA: Do you want to come in?

FARAH: No!

MONA: Are you leaving?

FARAH: Yes, um. I'm going to go . . . I mean.

MONA: Do you want an orange?

FARAH: What?

MONA: There's a tree in here.

FARAH: Oh. No. I'll be over by the mosque. (*She exits.*)

MONA: Okay, I'll find you.

> MONA *prostrates herself at the threshold of the house and then exits into it. A young man,* ARAM, *appears sitting at the gate of the house. He is played by the same actor who played the Young Man in Mona's dream.* MONA *reenters with an orange. She is startled when she sees* ARAM.

MONA: Oh. Who are you?

ARAM: Marry me.

MONA: What?

ARAM: Be my lover.

MONA: What are you talking about? Where's Farah?

ARAM: You should probably tell me your name first.

MONA: I don't even know who you are.

ARAM: Sure you do, I'm the man of your dreams.

MONA: Farah!

ARAM: She left.

MONA: What? Get down. You have no right cornering me like this. Farah!

FARAH (*off*): I'm not coming in there!

MONA: Farah, help!

FARAH (*entering*): What? What's wrong?

MONA: There's a man at the gate.

ARAM (*keeping his eyes fixed on* MONA): Hi Farah.

FARAH: Aram, what are you doing here?

ARAM: I was just introducing myself to your friend . . .

FARAH: He's only a boy that lives on my street.

ARAM: I am a man!

FARAH: A little boy with some whiskers. Don't let him scare you, Mona . . .

ARAM: Ah . . . Mona!

MONA: He didn't scare me. . . . I just didn't know who he was.

FARAH: Let's get out of here.

ARAM: Mona-Mona-Mona.

MONA: What?

FARAH: Aram, did you follow us?

ARAM: Mona-Mona-Mona . . .

MONA: Yes this is my name.

ARAM: Your name is Mona-Mona-Mona?

MONA: Just the one.

ARAM: You said "Mona-Mona-Mona" was your name.

MONA: No, I didn't. You said that.

ARAM: You said, this is my name.

FARAH: Aram, when are you going to grow up?

ARAM: I like "Mona-Mona-Mona."And that's what I'm going to call you.

MONA: Fine. But it's not my name.

FARAH: Aram, you followed us. We're leaving.

ARAM: Farah, I took one look at your friend and decided that destiny is not something to run away from. Nothing can hold it back or frustrate it. This one is mine.

FARAH: Mona, he's always talked like this. Everyone knows he's an idiot.

ARAM: Farah, you love me too much to think rationally.

FARAH: Yeah, right!

ARAM: I must admit that I'm only interested in your friend at the moment. Maybe if she and I don't work out, you and I can take another stab at it.

FARAH: Oh, you wish!

ARAM: Mona-Mona-Mona, she's still sorry that I stole a kiss from her.

FARAH: Mona, we were *ten years old,* playing in the street, and this little mulla comes up and plants one on my cheek.

He kisses in her direction.

FARAH: . . . When I'm not looking!

ARAM: Just think, Mona-Mona-Mona, you may be so lucky.

MONA: You think I'm going to kiss you?

ARAM: I know you will.

FARAH: Go home, Aram, before your father finds you here and kills you.

ARAM: I'm not really worried about my father right now. Besides, I'm interested in why the two of you are here.

A beat.

FARAH: This house belongs to one of Mona's relatives . . .

MONA: Farah . . .

ARAM: Really? You see, as I understand it, this piece of property was sacred to a certain reprehensible religious sect that all pious Muslims deem "unclean."And I know Farah isn't yet deep enough to be part of some esoteric cult . . .

FARAH: Watch it.

ARAM: So I'm trying to piece this together. When I first saw that face, I knew it was mine, from this world into the next — And now I see my radiant damsel in this den of moral darkness and I can't figure it out. How can this be unless you are . . . alas, Mona-Mona-Mona! . . . a Baha'i?

Silence.

MONA: I'm leaving. I didn't come here for more questions.

ARAM: Destiny, Mona-Mona-Mona! Think about it.

MONA *has left.*

FARAH: If you breathe a word of this!

ARAM: A little faith, my dear.

FARAH: Mona, wait up! (*She exits.*)

ARAM: Ciao. Have fun shopping. (*He hops down from his perch and walks towards the house.*) Shiraz, Shiraz, my city of roses! From what muck has this one sprung?

He grabs the orange MONA *has dropped and begins to peel it.* AQA HUSAYNI, *a religious cleric (a "mulla"), enters from the area of the mosque.*

AQA HUSAYNI (*calling*): Aram! Aram!

ARAM *panics and hides.* AQA HUSAYNI *stops and looks disdainfully at the house, then exits. End of scene.*

Scene 3 – Mahmudnizhad's Apartment

A modest apartment. Mona's FATHER, *Yadu'llah Mahmud-nizhad, is typing, one finger at a time on someone else's type-writer. He wears reading glasses.* MONA *enters with a shopping bag and stops just outside the door to the apartment. At the foot of the door is a long stem rose with a note. She picks up the flower and reads the note. She ponders the note, then goes to open the door. She hears the typing then pauses. She hides the rose by placing it down the front of her shirt. A thorn catches her skin and she winces and adjusts. She enters the room. Her* FATHER *looks up from typing, peering over his glasses to see her. They have a silent exchange.* MONA *then walks by him, leaning away a bit. She falters slightly in her stride, pricked by a hidden thorn. Her* FATHER *turns to watch her as she exits. He returns to typing.* MONA *reenters.*

FATHER: I've been thinking about your dream.

MONA: Yeah?

FATHER: Yes.

He nods his head significantly, and returns to his typing. Long pause while she waits for a further response. The FATHER *types.*

MONA: Well?

FATHER (*hand shooting up*): Mid-thought!

MONA: Sorry.

17

FATHER: Uh!

His hand again motions for silence; this is done without anger.
MONA goes to the kitchen and retrieves a bottle of Pepsi. She
returns, sits, drinks and waits. The FATHER finishes typing with
a two-finger flourish.

FATHER: Did you find what you were looking for?

MONA: You mean this? (*Indicating the bottle.*)

FATHER: Watch the carpet. No, I mean the house of the Báb.

MONA: How did you know?

FATHER: It's where I would have gone. So?

MONA: I'd rather not talk about it.

FATHER: Okay.

MONA: We went to the house and I went in and prayed, but
when I came out this guy was there and he kept staring at me
and he told me he wanted to marry me, and . . .

FATHER: So maybe this was the sign you were looking for?

MONA: I don't think so.

FATHER: I'm sure I don't know. (*He breaks and types.*) You know,
it's amazing that you even got the blue dress because . . . think
about it, you refused the first two dresses. This is a gift from
God, right?

MONA: I hadn't thought of that.

FATHER: Turning away a gift from God. Now that takes
courage.

MONA: But look at the option.

FATHER: Martyrdom. Would you like some tea? (*He goes to the kitchen.*)

MONA: Death, Dad! It was the death part that got my attention. No tea.

FATHER: Mona, I am not judging you. None of us knows what we would do under that circumstance.

MONA: I guess now I do. Maybe God was showing me last night.

FATHER: God was showing you that He loves you.

MONA: Dad, maybe he was showing me that I'm not strong enough. Maybe I'm only strong enough for service.

The FATHER *having reentered, stops. He is still for the first time in the scene.*

FATHER: Do you think it's easy to serve? We're not talking about tea.

MONA: I know that.

FATHER: Understand, Mona, that you are committing the rest of your life to helping others, encouraging others, suffering for others, sacrificing your time and your life . . .

MONA: I know, I know. But, you know, it was really the way the dress felt when I put it up to me. Bleah!

FATHER: And the black one?

MONA: It was just too heavy, Dad.

FATHER: It's a hard choice.

MONA: But it wasn't a real choice. You know how dreams are. Because if Baha'u'llah appeared to me right now and said, "Do this!" or "Do that!" that'd be different.

FATHER: In the dream the heart speaks.

MONA: Yeah, maybe that's it . . . But I don't know if I like that.

FATHER: Mona, do you want to die?

MONA: No, I mean, no, but that's not the point.

FATHER: It's exactly the point, you want to live!

MONA: Of course, I do.

FATHER: You like being alive!

> *The kettle whistles. Their neighbor,* MRS. KHUDAYAR, *unable to restrain herself any longer, knocks on their patio door.* MONA *goes to open it.*

MONA: Daddy, your water. Hello, Mrs. Khudayar.

MRS. KHUDAYAR (*entering*): Am I interrupting something?

FATHER: Mrs Khudayar, please come in. You'll have something to drink?

MRS. KHUDAYAR: No thank you.

FATHER: Mona and I were just discussing a wonderful dream that she had. Please I have just made some tea for myself.

MRS. KHUDAYAR: No, I couldn't. A dream? What kind of dream, Mona?

FATHER: Please. What's a cup of tea between neighbors?

MRS. KHUDAYAR: Thank you, just a cup then. You were saying, Mona?

MONA: Well, in the dream, uh . . . someone wanted to give me a gift. There were three dresses and I had to choose which one.

MRS. KHUDAYAR: Dresses?

MONA: Yeah, but . . .

MRS. KHUDAYAR: What did the labels say, Mona?

FATHER: Here is your tea, madam.

MRS. KHUDAYAR: Thank you. So which dress did you take, Mona? (*Low.*) Mona, you can tell me . . .

MONA: Well, it wasn't about the dresses really . . .

MRS. KHUDAYAR: I know, honey. You can tell me.

MONA: They were really about choices . . .

MRS. KHUDAYAR: Life choices, Mona?

MONA: Exactly. One was . . . uh, death . . .

MRS. KHUDAYAR: No. Don't want that one.

MONA: And another one was sorrow, a life of pain and suffering.

MRS. KHUDAYAR: Mona, if you just say yes to the boy, these dreams won't haunt you any more!

MONA: What are you talking about?

MRS. KHUDAYAR: Oh, as if . . . ! Oh! (*Aside to* MONA.) He doesn't know yet? Sorry, honey, my lips are sealed.

MONA: I don't think I understand.

MRS. KHUDAYAR: Of course not.

FATHER (*approaching*): Mrs. Khudayar, it's a wonderful dream, isn't it?

MRS. KHUDAYAR: I had a class once where we talked about psychology and dreaming. Sounded fascinating. Absolutely no practical benefit. Everything was death and sex, death and sex! Who needs to dream? It's our waking world, girl! Nice class though.

    MRS. KHUDAYAR *drinks.*

MONA: That's just what we were talking about.

MRS. KHUDAYAR: That's nice, Mona. It's very good to talk about things. The tea is delicious, Yadu'llah.

FATHER (*moving to kitchen*): Thank you. Would you like to bring some home?

MRS. KHUDAYAR: I wouldn't think of it. (*Aside.*) Mona, I saw your little present. At the door. Is he handsome?

MONA: What?

MRS. KHUDAYAR: Go! Run away with him, honey! Oh, to be young again!

FATHER (*off*): It's only a package of tea.

MRS. KHUDAYAR: We don't drink much tea anyway. (*Aside.*) Mona, when I was sixteen, I was already married with a loaf in the oven.

MONA: Yes, Mrs. Khudayar.

MRS. KHUDAYAR: You won't get any more beautiful, my dear.

FATHER (*bringing her package*): My neighbor of twelve years deserves so much more than this . . .

MRS. KHUDAYAR (*taking package, getting up to leave*): Thank you. Remember, Mona. Get out while you can.

MONA: Okay.

MRS. KHUDAYAR: Such a lovely rug! Oh, I almost forgot. Yadu'llah, they delivered this to the wrong address. I swear to you, it arrived unsealed. Those goons with the Revolutionary Guard can't admit that they're censoring the mail so they try to put it off on me.

FATHER: We have consummate trust in you, Mrs. Khudayar.

MRS. KHUDAYAR: That's your problem, Mahmudnizhad, you trust too much! But they're watching you!

FATHER: Thank you for your concern, Mrs. Khudayar.

MRS. KHUDAYAR: I'm just letting you know

FATHER: You didn't finish your tea. Please take it with you . . .

MRS. KHUDAYAR: I'll bring the cup back.

FATHER: As you always do.

MRS. KHUDAYAR (*exiting*): Goodbye.

FATHER & MONA: Goodbye, Mrs. Khudayar.

FATHER: Now tell me, cause I'm dying to know! Who was it from?

MONA: Oh, the letter?

FATHER: The flower.

MONA: Dad! How do you know about that?

FATHER: You don't have to tell me.

MONA: I don't hide things from you, Dad.

FATHER: You don't have to.

MONA: I don't know. I mean, I'm not sure.

She exits. He watches her exit, then turns to the typewriter and pulls out the paper, signs it and begins stuffing it in an envelope. MONA *reenters.*

FATHER: So what does it all mean, do you think?

She hands him the flower.

FATHER: That must have hurt.

MONA: Well, I chose service to mankind. Now it's just how best to serve.

She drinks some of her Pepsi.

FATHER: Ah! From the "man of your dreams"

MONA: Exactly!

FATHER: So this is from him?

MONA: How could he know where I live? And we only went to the shop.

FATHER: Are you afraid of him?

MONA: Not afraid.

FATHER (*getting up*): Well, my dear, answers come in very different forms. Here.

MONA: Thanks.

He hands her the envelope he has sealed, which she opens. He gets up puts the rose in the Pepsi bottle and exits.

MONA: Dad, is getting married a kind of service?

FATHER (*off*): Getting married!

MONA: Not that I'm — just hypothetically.

FATHER: Hmm. Could be.

MONA *reads the letter, puts it down.*

MONA: Dad! Why didn't you tell me this?!

FATHER (*reentering*): It took me an eternity to come up with that. I couldn't just blurt it out.

MONA: Yeah, but you could have given me a hint or something.

FATHER: Honey, this is an official request from the Baha'i community. I was asked, in my capacity as secretary, only to type it up.

MONA: So this is is it? Teaching is how I serve.

FATHER: It's a good start.

MONA *is absorbed in thought.*

FATHER: When did your mother say she'd be home?

MONA: She didn't.

FATHER (*low*): Mrs. Khudayar always seems to find us at the strangest times. I'm joking or carrying on, shouting . . .

MONA: Paper walls.

FATHER: Hmm. So who do you think the young man was?

MONA: Huh?

FATHER: In the dream.

MONA: Oh. I don't know. I don't remember his face. Exactly. I think I'm confusing him with someone else that I've seen.

FATHER: Yeah?

MONA: Then Mom was there. He reminded me of you. But younger. (*She exits.*)

FATHER: You have to look at this dream as a great gift, Mona. Service to mankind. The dress was blue. The young man was dashing.

MONA (*off*): I didn't say "dashing."

FATHER: You said he looked like me!

Music begins to play loudly from the other room. MONA *reenters with the shopping bag she brought in earlier. With a flourish, she pulls a blue dress out of the bag.*

FATHER: A-haaaaaaa! Very nice.

MONA *holds the dress up to herself and begins to dance. Her father begins to dance along with her. Soon thereafter, Mona's* MOTHER *enters with food. They try to get her to join in, but she is very distracted. The* FATHER *exits to shut off the music.*

MONA: Hi Mama. What have you got? Is this for me?

FATHER: Farkhundih? (*He reenters.*)

MONA (*jumping onto the couch with a bag*): You know, Dad, I'm happy to stay at home and eat chocolate.

FATHER: Farkhundih, are you okay?

The MOTHER *has dropped her other bags and now trembles.*

MONA: Mom, what's wrong?

MOTHER: Where in hell are we living??!! (*She covers her mouth in shame.*)

FATHER: Please, my dear, sit down.

MOTHER: Hate. Hate. Everywhere, hate. These people, they hate. They're filled with hate, and I don't know why we stay.

FATHER: What happened to you?

MOTHER: I was coming back from the market with the bags and it was windy. The wind was blowing my chador, and this . . . this man, this mulla, stops me and shouts at me for not having my neck covered up, I'm unchaste and desecrating the name of Islam.

MONA: Did he know you were a Baha'i?

MOTHER: He said if he were my husband, he would have me whipped.

MONA: What did you do?

MOTHER: Mona, what could I do? Nothing. I have no power. Who am I? I'm nothing to him. Nothing.

   Mona's FATHER *embraces his wife. A beat.*

FATHER: Farkhundih, what was his name?

MOTHER: His name? I don't know what his name is . . . why?

FATHER (*breaking away from her*): Could you point him out if you saw him again?

MOTHER: Yadu'llah, what are you asking me?

FATHER: Answer me, would you know him if you saw him?

MOTHER: Yes, but Yadu'llah, he's a mulla. He's a powerful man.

FATHER: I'm going to track down Mr. Mulla if it's the last thing I ever do . . . (*He picks up the phone.*)

MOTHER: Yadu'llah, you're a Baha'i for God's sake!

FATHER: I'm going to track down Mr. Mulla and I'm gonna . . .

MOTHER: We don't seek revenge!

FATHER: I'm gonna thank him!

MOTHER: Yadu'llah!

MONA: Mom, you fall for him every time!

MOTHER (*to* FATHER): Why you . . . !

FATHER (*into phone*): Operator, give me Mr. Mulla on the phone right this instant. What? You don't know who Mr. Mulla is?! That fearless protector of the chastity of women?! (*Hanging up the phone.*) I need to find Mr. Mulla, and to thank him for setting my wife straight, for setting me straight and reminding me of my duty as a good Iranian citizen to beat my wife into line. Woman! You! Come to your husband this instant!

MONA *is laughing.*

MOTHER (*getting up, moving away from him*): Yadu'llah! What are you doing?

FATHER (*to* MONA): You! You, saucy girl! Give me that! (*He takes her chocolate.*) It's time I showed the women in this house who's who! (*Breaking off a piece of chocolate and slamming it on the table in front of his wife.*) Take that! Huh? How do you like that, woman?!

MOTHER (*eating*): Oh, I like it!

FATHER: You what?! Then take another! (*He slams down another piece of chocolate.*) And, you, saucy girl! I'll teach you to laugh! (*He slams down a piece for* MONA.) Oh, yes, I need to thank Mr. Mulla! And, by God, my women will thank Mr. Mulla too!

MONA & MOTHER: Thank you, Mr. Mulla!

FATHER: More lashings to go around! (*Slamming down the rest of the chocolate.*) Oh, Mr. Mulla, how your lash has made everything right in the world! It just makes me want some too!

The three of them are shouting, eating, laughing and slamming the table. Pounding on the door. Instantly, they are silent. MRS. KHUDAYAR *pokes her head in.*

MRS. KHUDAYAR: Am I interrupting something?

She shows her empty cup. End of scene.

Scene 4 – A Mosque in Shiraz & Mona's room

The chanting of a prayer is heard. The large picture frame is center stage. In front of the frame, a man prostrates himself. He rises and turns. He is AQA HUSAYNI *from Scene 2. He speaks as if addressing a congregation.*

AQA HUSAYNI: Praise be to God! We stand today at the threshold of a new Iran! How far we have come in so short a time. We were cursed with a tyrannical government, now the love of the Islamic Revolution is spreading! In the grips of the corrupt powers of the West, now an independent Iran once again shows its face! Ruled by a cruel, conniving and concupiscent despot, now the Shah is dead!! The Shah is dead and Ayatu'l-láh Khomeini has returned, leading us into this new day, into this new Iran! Praise be to God!

Scene shift. MONA *enters, carrying the blue dress from the previous scene. She comes behind the frame, looking into it, as if assessing the fit of the dress in a mirror. After a moment, she closes her eyes, breathing deeply. Scene shift.*

AQA HUSAYNI: We are honored today with the presence of an esteemed brother in God's revolution, the Religious Magistrate of the Revolutionary Court. Please welcome Ayatu'lláh Qazá'í.

He exits. The doors to the back of the house fly open. The RELI-GIOUS MAGISTRATE *enters. He is played by the same actor that has portrayed the Young Man and Áram, but he now wears a beard and a large turban. He walks straight towards* MONA, *who has opened her eyes with a start. They are locked in a stare as he comes closer. He walks until he is just opposite her through the mirror frame. He puts on a pair of eyeglasses, and her stare is broken as if the vision of him has vanished. She breaks away. He turns.*

MAGISTRATE: Let us talk about "Baha'i." (*Pause.*) Baha'i says it is a religion. Islam says Baha'i is a political sect. The Twelfth Imam has returned, Baha'i says. My friends, if the Twelfth Imam had returned, I should not be standing here. He should be here, and I should be on the floor in humility like you. But here I am, and I ask: Where is Imam? (*A beat.*) But wait, you may say. Baha'is aren't so bad, you may say. You see them around. They seem nice, you say. Before you know it, you're seeking them out. Meeting them in back alleys, and they begin to fill you up with their poison! Filling your cup! The poison is sweet, they say! Drink it down, my friends, BUT KNOW!!! God reads your heart, even as I read the Qur'an! (*With a thick guttural Arabic pronunciation*) "Házá va enna letagheyna lashara ma'ábe, Jahannama yaslavanahá fabe'ass-al Mehádo!"[1] This is what God has revealed! This plague will be eradicated from this land. Starting now. And you will do it.

During the Magistrate's speech, MONA, *now wearing the dress, has returned to stand before the frame. Chanting begins as the* MAGISTRATE *finishes. He turns and prostrates himself, in effect, bowing before* MONA. MONA *addresses herself in the mirror, practicing her delivery.*

MONA: My name is Mona. I was asked to come and act as your teacher. I've never done this before so . . . maybe we can start by getting to know each other better.

---

1 Qur'an 38:55-56, *translated*: This is so! And for the transgressors will be an evil return! Hell! Where they will burn, and worst is that place to rest!

The MAGISTRATE *rises and goes.* MONA's *attention seems distracted by something she sees in the mirror. Her hand goes up to her head. She puts her fingers in her hair and pulls out a strand to examine.*

MONA: O my God.

End of scene.

Scene 5 – A Public Secondary School for Girls in Shiraz

A SCHOOL SECRETARY *is seated behind a desk. She sharpens pencils from a pencil box. She stops, adjusts her head scarf, making sure all the hair is out of sight, starts sharpening again. An annoyingly loud* VOICE *comes over a loudspeaker.*

VOICE: Uh . . . Mr. Kermani?

SECRETARY (*shouting*): Mr. Kermani is not here today!

VOICE: Well, where is he?

SECRETARY: I don't know where he is!

VOICE: Uh . . . .

SECRETARY: Can I help you?

VOICE: Uh . . . (*Long pause.*) . . . no.

The intercom goes off. The SECRETARY *makes a face. She pulls a smaller pencil out to sharpen, goes to the door, looks both ways, then closes it. Going back to the desk, she pulls out a make-up compact and begins to line her eyes with the small pencil. She looks in the mirror and frowns. She begins putting on blush when there's a loud knocking on the door.*

AQA HUSAYNI (*off*): Ya Allah!

The SECRETARY *is startled and spills the box of pencils and makeup effects.*

SECRETARY: Oh! Oh, no!

AQA HUSAYNI (*off*): Ya Allah!

SECRETARY: Hold on! I'm coming! (*In a frenzy, she picks up the makeup and then goes to the door.*) Oh, can I . . . ? Hello, um . . . . excuse me! (*She adjusts her scarf and clothing.*) Can I help you?

AQA HUSAYNI (*barging in*): Sister, why was the door not left open?

SECRETARY: Your honor, I was using . . . the um . . . you know . . .

AQA HUSAYNI: Where is the principal?

SECRETARY: Why? I didn't do anything wrong.

AQA HUSAYNI: I need to speak with him. Now.

SECRETARY: Well, he's not in.

AQA HUSAYNI: Then you'll have to help me.

SECRETARY: Oh?

AQA HUSAYNI: Sister, what's wrong with your cheeks?

SECRETARY: My cheeks?

AQA HUSAYNI: They're red.

SECRETARY: Oh! I'm . . . blushing. Yes, I'm not used to being disturbed . . . I mean pleasantly disturbed, by such a . . . I mean, a man of such . . .

AQA HUSAYNI: Yes?

SECRETARY: Robust-ness.

AQA HUSAYNI: Robust-ness? (*He smiles.*) Hmm. Sister, show me your files.

SECRETARY: My what?

AQA HUSAYNI: The files. The school registration files.

SECRETARY: Oh, of course, of course.

> *They exit. Switch to* MR. ALIZADEH's *English class with* MONA, FARAH *and some other girls. All the girls wear thick clothing and head scarves. They speak the "English" phrases with a Persian accent.*

MR. ALIZADEH: And again . . .

CLASS: "I would like to buy a kidney pie for my wife."

MR. ALIZADEH: Not "vife"! Wa-wa-wa. Wwwwwwife! Speak it like an Arab!

CLASS: "I would like to buy a kidney pie for my wife."

MR. ALIZADEH: And again . . .

CLASS: "I would like to buy a kidney pie for my wife."

MR. ALIZADEH: Now what about this word ordering? Does someone have it? Yes, Miss Mahmudnizhad.

MONA: The subject comes first.

MR. ALIZADEH: And what is that subject . . . Miss Ja'fari?

FARAH (*breaking out of a daydream*): Sorry, sir?

MR. ALIZADEH: The subject?

FARAH: Yes, the subject, sir . . . the subject is "I."

MR. ALIZADEH: Correct. Now, class, is it necessary to include the word "I"?

CLASS: Yeeeeesss.

MR. ALIZADEH: Are you sure? Miss Ja'fari.

FARAH: Yes, sir.

MR. ALIZADEH: Class, is it not like Persian where you can just add the pronoun if you feel like it?

CLASS: Nnnoooo.

MR. ALIZADEH: The English are very impatient, you know. They don't want to wait til the end of the sentence before they figure out who's doing what. The subject is first. Miss Mahmudnizhad, please continue, what is next?

MONA: Next comes the verb.

MR. ALIZADEH: The verb comes next! Exactly, those English are so impatient they need to know right away what's happening and who's doing it. Where's the poetry in that, I ask you?! Huh? Huh? Persian, you see, is a circle. You need the whole of it to understand any of it, but the English, the English are in such a hurry, they hear the headline, the "who" and the "what" and, bam, they're off to colonize another part of the world, and you're not even finished with your sentence!

MONA *raises her hand.*

MR. ALIZADEH: Yes, Miss Mahmudnizhad.

MONA: Then why teach?

MR. ALIZADEH: Excuse me?

MONA: Why teach English? Why teach something that you don't care about?

Pause. The SECRETARY's *voice comes over the intercom speaker.*

SECRETARY: Mr. Alizadeh?

MR. ALIZADEH (*shouting at the intercom speaker*): What do you want, disembodied voice?!

The class laughs.

SECRETARY: Mr. Alizadeh, please come down to the main office.

MR. ALIZADEH: Disembodied voice! I finally get a student to ask a question and you interrupt!

SECRETARY: There's a man here who wants to see you. He's a . . . um . . . . a man. He wants to see you.

MR. ALIZADEH: Okay, that's a big help.

The class laughs again.

SECRETARY: What was that?

MR. ALIZADEH: I'm a-comin! Miss Mahmudnizhad, I leave you to watch over the class while I'm gone.

He exits. FARAH *sighs.*

FARAH: It's a shame.

MONA: What?

FARAH: That he's so old.

MONA: He's not that old. Do you think he's divorced?

FARAH: Mona, since when are you so interested?

MONA: I was just saying . . .

Another GIRL *nearby has been listening.*

GIRL: My friend has a cousin and she said that his father is sixty-five years older than his wife.

FARAH: What?!

GIRL: I swear.

FARAH: And they had a kid?

GIRL: When the guy was one hundred years old.

A beat.

MONA: How?

They break into laughter.

MONA: Mr. Alizadeh doesn't sound bad at all after that.

The girls stop laughing and stare at MONA. *Shift to the main office where the* SECRETARY, *disturbed, continues sharpening pencils.*

SECRETARY: I hate it when he does that.

MR. ALIZADEH *enters and approaches her.*

MR. ALIZADEH: Yes, my love, how can I help you?

SECRETARY: Mr. Alizadeh, I wish you wouldn't shout at me when I page you.

MR. ALIZADEH: It's the anger of passion, I assure you.

SECRETARY: Mr. Alizadeh, there is a religious gentleman in the other room.

MR. ALIZADEH: Really? Gentleness and religion mingle so seldom these days.

SECRETARY: Sshh.

AQA HUSAYNI *enters.*

SECRETARY: Mr. Alizadeh, this gentleman is from the Revolutionary Court.

AQA HUSAYNI: Ya Allah.

MR. ALIZADEH: Hi.

SECRETARY: He is concerned about the number of students in this school that belong to the Baha'i sect.

MR. ALIZADEH: How many is that now? One?

AQA HUSAYNI: One too many.

MR. ALIZADEH: Okay. So what harm has this child done?

AQA HUSAYNI: I'd prefer to speak of this in private.

He steps outside of the office. MR. ALIZADEH *hesitates, gives a look to the* SECRETARY *and then exits. Shift back to the classroom. The girls are quietly reading.* MONA *starts to play with her hair. She pulls out a strand from underneath her head scarf and looks at it. As she does this, a* MALE FIGURE *is silently climbing through the classroom window.*

MONA: Farah. Look.

FARAH: What? (*Looking closer.*) O Wow! Congratulations, Mona, you have your first grey hair!

GIRL: Is that all?

MONA: Is that all? My mother was grey by the time she was thirty!

FARAH: I already have half-a-dozen.

GIRL: So who's going to notice now we're wearing these nasty scarves all the time?

MONA: I notice! It means I'm getting old!

MALE FIGURE: Don't believe it, Mona!

The girls scream. The MALE FIGURE *comes forward. It's* ARAM.

FARAH: Aram! What are you doing here?!

ARAM: Mona, I would love you even shriveled up and decayed with only wisps of white hair.

MONA: Shut up! Shut up!!

FARAH: Aram! Get out! Get out! You can't be here.

ARAM: No, listen, quiet down. I have to talk to you.

FARAH: Get out!

ARAM: Mona, I have to talk to you.

MONA: I have nothing to say to you, Aram! You have to leave!

A beat. ARAM *appears shocked.*

ARAM: Who is he, Mona? Who is he?

MONA: What?

ARAM: The other man. Tell me who he is and what he does for you! Whatever it is, I'll do you better.

A slight beat.

MONA: He gave me a dress.

ARAM: Is that all? Mona-Mona-Mona, I'll give you three!

FARAH (*coming and swinging a pointing stick at him*): Get out, Aram! Get out! . . . .

ARAM: Easy, Farah! Easy! Wait, I need to say something to Mona. It's important. Ow!

FARAH: Get out!

ARAM: Here, at least let me write it down!

She drives him back toward the window. Scene shift. MR. ALIZADEH *reenters followed by* AQA HUSAYNI.

MR. ALIZADEH: Listen, Aqa, let's drop the pretense. That girl is as much a spy for Israel as I am. You're threatened by her religion so you come up with these conspiracy theories.

AQA HUSAYNI: The Baha'i sect is an illegal organization in this land and that girl is actively propagating it.

MR. ALIZADEH: Teaching a class of six year olds.

AQA HUSAYNI: Poisoning their minds against Islam.

MR. ALIZADEH: If you ask me, the clergy is the real threat to Islam.

SECRETARY: Mr. Alizadeh!

MR. ALIZADEH: What? Why do they come to me? Who am I? I'm a foreign-language teacher. What do I know about international politics? Why do they need my approval to kick out one harmless girl from school?

AQA HUSAYNI: It has to do with a certain teacher's union you belong to.

MR. ALIZADEH: Oh . . . that.

AQA HUSAYNI: Now, Alizadeh, as you say, let's drop the pretense. You stand there with your cocky, Marxist politics and hollow European values, and think you can judge the rest of the world from your perch. But you are not my judge, Alizadeh. We're in the midst of a revolution . . . The Judgment, when the righteous and the sinners are separated, and those in the middle — who fail to take a side — are hacked in two by the sword of God. (*A beat.*) But what I'd like to know is if this girl is expelled, the teachers will show up for school tomorrow.

MR. ALIZADEH: Why should that concern you, Aqa? Are you not a man of principle?

AQA HUSAYNI: I need to know that the schools will be open tomorrow.

MR. ALIZADEH: The people who unlock the doors are not in our union.

AQA HUSAYNI: Alizadeh, you should know that this is not my only recourse to action.

MR. ALIZADEH: What if you just let the girl alone?

AQA HUSAYNI: The girl is part of a much larger problem and I think you know what I mean.

He smiles. MR. ALIZADEH *exits. Switch back to classroom.* FARAH *is standing by the window, holding it shut as* ARAM *pounds on it.*

GIRL (*in a hushed voice*): Quick, Farah! He's coming.

FARAH *runs back to her seat.* ARAM *has stopped pounding.*

MR. ALIZADEH (*entering*): Okay, where were we?

He is distracted and flips through some pages of a book. ARAM *slips a piece of paper through the window.* MONA *sees it. The signal to change classes sounds.*

MR. ALIZADEH: So much for that. Have a nice day.

The students pack up to leave. MONA *covertly walks over to the window and picks up the note.*

MR. ALIZADEH: Miss Mahmudnizhad . . .

MONA: Yes, sir?

MR. ALIZADEH (*hesitates, then begins to write a note*): Can you tell your father to call me?

MONA: My father?

MR. ALIZADEH: Yes. Here is my number.

MONA: Is it something I did?

MR. ALIZADEH: Nothing. Just ask him to call me. I need to talk to him.

MONA: Okay.

MR. ALIZADEH: We'll see you tomorrow.

MONA: Bye.

> MR. ALIZADEH *exits.* *Everyone else has gone.* MONA *looks at Alizadeh's note, then at Aram's. She covers her mouth.* FARAH *reenters.*

FARAH: Mona, are you coming?

> MONA *rushes out.*

FARAH: Mona, wait! What's wrong? Hey! Wait for me!

> FARAH *exits. End of scene.*

Scene 6 – The Site of the House of the Báb

Some grievers enter and walk around the space, looking right and left, searching. They help one another sort through the mess, deal with the difficulty. MONA *and* FARAH *enter.* MONA *looks out over the ruins of the house of the Báb.*

MONA: I can't see it. I can't see it. Really. Farah, it's not there.

FARAH: I know, Mona.

MONA: No, I mean it's not there. I can't see it.

FARAH (*with gentleness*): Mona, this is the third time we've walked around the lot and you keep saying you don't see it. What am I supposed to say? The house isn't there anymore. That's why you don't see it.

MONA: No. No. I mean I can't see it. In my head, it's not there. I'm looking for the picture. I should have the picture. I'm trying to remember but I can't see it. It's gone.

FARAH: Okay, so you don't want to turn around, there's a group of religious men coming this way.

Some men have entered, including AQA HUSAYNI *and* ARAM, *dressed in a clerical outfit. He appears uncomfortable in his new apparel. The men survey the site and* AQA HUSAYNI *is pointing out other houses in the area.*

FARAH: Maybe we should leave.

MONA: What more can they do to me, Farah? (*She turns.*) Wait, isn't that Aram?

FARAH: Where? O my God. What's he, following us again?

MONA: Why is he dressed that way?

FARAH: I don't know. Aram!

AQA HUSAYNI (*to* ARAM): Do you know those girls?

FARAH: Going to a parade, Aram?

ARAM: They're just some girls.

AQA HUSAYNI: Come.

ARAM: Wait, father. (*He walks back towards* FARAH *and* MONA.)

MONA: Here he comes.

FARAH: Aram, my friend has no interest in you so leave her alone

MONA: Farah . . .

ARAM (*over the top, to* FARAH): You! You have something to say to me, you stupid girl!

FARAH: Whoa!

ARAM (*low*): Mona, get out of your home. (*Loud.*) Be happy I don't have a stick!

MONA: What? What are you talking about, Aram?

ARAM: You must learn to respect the man!

FARAH: Excuse me?

ARAM (*low*): Mona, your family is in danger. (*Loud.*) You will learn to respect the man! (*Low.*) Tonight. Tonight. (*Loud.*) Be thankful these respectable gentlemen are here, or I'd show you what I'm talking about!

ARAM *looks at* MONA *furtively and walks away. The men exit, laughing.*

FARAH: That was the strangest thing that I've ever seen.

MONA: What was he talking about?

FARAH: I have no idea. Maybe he really is crazy.

MONA: He was trying to warn me. My family.

FARAH: What does he know? I mean, he's just Aram . . .

MONA: Was that his father?

FARAH: This is getting a little weird. Are you ready to go yet?

MONA: No. I'm going in.

FARAH: In there?

MONA: Do you want to come?

FARAH: I don't think I should.

MONA *walks into the ruins.*

FARAH: Be careful, Mona, there might be glass.

A moment where MONA *just stands still.*

MONA: O my God.

FARAH: What? Mona, are you okay?

MONA: O my God.

FARAH: O my God — what? What's wrong?

MONA: It's here.

FARAH: What?

MONA: Farah, it's here. It's still here! I feel it!

FARAH: You feel what?

MONA: It's here. No, no, this is only rubble. (*She laughs.*) Farah, do you get it? Don't you see? They didn't destroy it! Farah, look at them! Look at everyone! Do you see them? That's why! No, they didn't touch it! They didn't touch this place. This is holy rubble, Farah. This is holy r — Oh, no!! They chopped it down!!

    MONA *moves out of sight briefly.*

FARAH: Chopped it down? Mona, what are you talking about? Will you please tell me because I have not understood a single word you've spoken since we've been here and what with Aram coming in here with that outfit and freaking out like he's on drugs, I think I might be the one who's losing it!

MONA: Aha!

FARAH: Aha-what?! Mona, where did you go? I can't see you.

MONA: They forgot something.

FARAH: What?

MONA: Catch.

    MONA *tosses* FARAH *an orange. End of scene.*

Scene 7 – Mahmudnizhad's Apartment

MONA *enters quietly. She looks at her shoes, then at the floor, and hesitates.*

MONA: Mama?

MOTHER (*off*): Mona?

MONA: Mama. I don't wish to take off my shoes.

MOTHER (*entering*): Mona, are you okay?

MONA: I'm fine. Is it okay if I come into the house with my shoes on?

MOTHER: Did you know there's been more violence? Your father went to find you.

MONA: Do you know about the House?

MOTHER: Oh, Mona, it's awful . . . just awful.

MONA: Mama, my shoes . . .

MOTHER: Mona, I could care less about your shoes! You could have been hurt!

MONA: These shoes have tread on holy rubble, Mama.

MOTHER: Oh. . . .

MONA: Don't be sad, listen. I stood there. There's still something there, something they haven't touched.

MOTHER: But Mona, they destroyed the most sacred place we have.

MONA: I know, but don't you see? If none of this had happened, we wouldn't see how much love we have, or how strong we can be. God took away these outer things to show us the real stuff inside.

MOTHER: God didn't destroy the house. It was a group of fanatics! A group of thugs and thieves!

MONA: Mama, I hear you, but I didn't see them. I only saw the Baha'is. And the Baha'is were beautiful.

MOTHER: Why are we here? Why do we have to stay here in this hole? Why didn't we get out while we could? O Mona, where is your father? Anything could happen out there, he could get hurt . . . He went looking for you. Oh, no, someone had to stay behind! It couldn't be him! No, me! Always me!

MONA: Mama. (*She hugs her* MOTHER.)

MOTHER: O Mona, why does God put us through this?

Silence. MONA *starts giving her* MOTHER *a long, wet noisy kiss on the cheek.*

MOTHER: Mona, stop it! That's horrible. I don't want to laugh. Stop! I don't want to laugh!

MONA *continues until they are both laughing.* MONA *breaks. A knock at the door. They are still.*

MOTHER: Is that your father?

MONA: Why would he knock?

MOTHER: O Mona, get that. I'm going to look like a raccoon. (*She tries to sop off her makeup.*)

MONA (*opening door*): Mrs. Khudayar.

MRS. KHUDAYAR (*hugging her*): Mona, you're home! Oh, honey, I'm so glad you're safe. Don't scare us like that again.

MONA: Mama, did you tell the whole neighborhood?

MOTHER: I didn't tell anyone.

MONA: Then how did you . . . ?

MRS. KHUDAYAR: Oh . . . Mona, I just know, okay? I just know these things. The important thing is that you're back. (*She turns to leave. To someone off.*) Can I help you?

MR. ALIZADEH (*off*): Oh, no, I think this is the place. Thank you. (*He approaches the door.*)

MONA: Mr. Alizadeh?

MR. ALIZADEH: Miss Mahmudnizhad, it's . . . uh, good to see you. I forgot which apartment it was.

MONA: It's okay, Mrs. Khudayar, this is my teacher.

MRS. KHUDAYAR: Do teachers make house calls these days?

MR. ALIZADEH: I am just hoping to speak to the father.

MRS. KHUDAYAR: Well, he's not here. That is, I assume he's not here . . . there. I don't think he's home. Mona, is your father home?

MONA: No . . .

MRS. KHUDAYAR: See. I'm leaving now. (*She exits.*)

MR. ALIZADEH: Maybe I can come back.

MONA: Was it something important?

MR. ALIZADEH: Did you give him that piece of paper?

MONA: Oh, that note! I completely forgot, Mr. Alizadeh. But I haven't even seen him . . .

MR. ALIZADEH: It's okay, Miss Mahmudnizhad. When will your father be home?

MONA: I'm not sure . . . Um . . . he went out. Maybe you can come in.

MR. ALIZADEH: That would not be appropriate.

MONA: No, it's okay, my mother is here.

MR. ALIZADEH: Your mother?

MONA: Yes. Please come in.

MR. ALIZADEH (*entering*): Thank you. (*A slight beat.*) Hello Farkhundih.

MOTHER (*coolly*): Hello.

MR. ALIZADEH: You are looking well.

MOTHER: Thank you.

MONA: You know each other?

MOTHER: Mona, take his coat. I'll get him something to drink.

MR. ALIZADEH: Oh . . .

MONA: Would you like to sit?

MR. ALIZADEH: Uh . . . Thank you.

A beat.

MR. ALIZADEH: Nice rug.

MOTHER: Wedding gift.

Silence.

MONA: So I take it you two have met?

MR. ALIZADEH: Your father and I went to school together. That's how we met.

MONA: Really? Where?

MOTHER: Mona, come get the teacher his tea.

MR. ALIZADEH: You know, it's getting kind of late. Maybe it's better if he just called me.

MONA (*uncertain where her duty lies*): Oh . . . well . . . um. Here's your tea. If you want it.

MR. ALIZADEH: Oh. Thank you. (*Pause.*) Do you know when he's going to be back?

MONA: Mom, do you know?

MOTHER: I have no idea.

MR. ALIZADEH: It's just really important that I talk to him.

MOTHER (*turning to face him for the first time*): What is the message? Maybe you can tell us. Maybe we can tell him.

MR. ALIZADEH: Well . . .

MOTHER: Unless it's too delicate for female ears.

MR. ALIZADEH: No, it's not that.

MOTHER: Unless maybe we women are unable to deal with the complex ideas . . .

MR. ALIZADEH: Farkhundih . . .

MOTHER: Or the grave responsibilities.

MR. ALIZADEH: Very well. It concerns you all.

MONA: What is it?

MR. ALIZADEH: This afternoon, we had a visit from a certain mulla who was placing pressure on the school to have your daughter expelled.

MONA: Really? Me?

MR. ALIZADEH: Miss Mahmudnizhad, you have to know that no free thinker is safe in this world.

MOTHER: What was the reason he gave?

MR. ALIZADEH: Her involvement in your religious activities.

MONA: Really? What activities?

MR. ALIZADEH: He mentioned that you were teaching a Baha'i children's class.

MONA: The children's class? Really? Did he mention me by name?

MR. ALIZADEH: Yes.

MONA: Wow!

MOTHER: When was this?

MR. ALIZADEH: This was during school today.

MOTHER: And . . .

MR. ALIZADEH: And?

MOTHER: Is she expelled?

MR. ALIZADEH: No. The little clout that I have in our school prevailed. For the moment.

A beat.

MOTHER: Thank you.

MR. ALIZADEH: It's only for the moment. What we're dealing with here is an organized campaign to exterminate your religion.

MOTHER: *My* religion?

MR. ALIZADEH: Yes. And there's nothing I can do about that.

MONA *has been wandering around, absorbed in thought.*

MONA: Mama, this means I might be persecuted.

MOTHER: It's nothing to be proud of.

MONA: Yeah, but they actually mentioned me by name. The Mulla came in and said: (*With a thick Arabic accent.*) Bismulláh'u'l-rahmán-i-rahím! Mona Mahmudnizhad must not be allowed to stay at this school!

MR. ALIZADEH: Miss Mahmudnizhad, I don't believe this is a matter to make light of. You and your family, as long as you are here, are in danger.

MONA: Mr. Alizadeh, I understand why you might think that, but really . . . we're okay.

MR. ALIZADEH: No, in fact you're not. You are actually in very great danger. Mrs. Mahmudnizhad, please have your husband call me.

MONA: Mr. Alizadeh?

MR. ALIZADEH: Yes?

MONA: Do you want me to tell you how I know we will be okay?

MOTHER: Mona, will you please bring me that cup?

MONA: Just a second. Mr. Alizadeh.

MOTHER: Mona.

MONA: Mom, Mr. Alizadeh came all the way over here to share his concern with us. I feel obligated to tell him why I feel there is no need for that concern. Mr. Alizadeh . . . (*Pause.*) I had a dream not too long ago . . .

MOTHER: Mona, I'm sure Mr. Alizadeh doesn't want to hear about your dream.

MONA: Mama, I feel we owe an explanation to Mr. Alizadeh.

MOTHER: Mona, you don't have to explain yourself to him.

MONA: Mama, please. It's my dream. I want to share it with my teacher.

The MOTHER *is silent.*

MONA: Mr. Alizadeh, would you like to hear my dream?

A beat.

MR. ALIZADEH: Sure.

MONA: Good. In my dream, God offered me three choices. But they appeared as three dresses. The first was red, and it meant that I should die for my beliefs. I did not take that dress. The second was black and it meant suffering. I didn't take that dress either. The last was blue and it meant service, and that was the one that I chose. So, you see, I know I'm safe. I understand it might be hard for you to accept this dream because you are not a Baha'i, but to me, Mr. Alizadeh. That dream was more real than you sitting there in front of me.

A beat.

MR. ALIZADEH: Thank you for sharing your dream with me, Miss Mahmudnizhad.

MONA: You're welcome. (*She smiles to her* MOTHER.)

MOTHER: Mr. Alizadeh, would you mind waiting a moment on the patio?

MR. ALIZADEH: Uh . . .

MOTHER: Please. Just a moment. It's a nice view of the city.

MR. ALIZADEH: Okay.

MOTHER: Please. (*She closes the door behind him.*) Mona, I would like you to go to your room.

MONA: My room?

MOTHER: Yes.

MONA: Mom, I'm sixteen years old.

MOTHER: Mona, you disobeyed me.

MONA: Mother. I was teaching my teacher.

MOTHER: You disobeyed me!

Tears begin to well up in MONA'*s eyes.*

MOTHER: Go to your room.

MONA: But Mama . . .

MOTHER: Mona, do you think that I am stupid? That I say things for no reason?

MONA: No.

MOTHER: Do you think that it was for nothing that I asked you not to tell him your dream?

MONA: He's my teacher . . .

MOTHER: Fine, he's your teacher. Let him teach you English. But you are my daughter and you will obey me.

MONA: But, Mama, he's my teacher.

MOTHER: He's dangerous. (*Pause.*) Go to your room.

> MONA *leaves. The* MOTHER *takes a moment to regain her composure. As she is moving to the patio door, the* FATHER *enters.*

MOTHER: Yadu'llah!

FATHER: Farkhundih. What's wrong? Why are you upset? Is it Mona?

MOTHER: We have a guest.

MONA: Daddy??

FATHER: Mona?! Is that you?

MONA: It's me.

He falls to the ground and kisses it.

MOTHER: Yadu'llah. We have a guest.

FATHER: A guest? Mona is now a guest? Mona, where are you? Come out here so I can see you.

MONA: I can't.

FATHER: Why not?

MONA: I'm not supposed to come out.

FATHER: Who says?

MONA: Mama.

MOTHER: Yadu'llah.

FATHER: Farkhundih, what's wrong? Our daughter is back. You don't know what I've been through tonight. Going through the streets, the alleys. You don't know. Finally, all I could do to keep my sanity was to give her up. I did! I gave her up. I gave her to God! Farkhundih, you don't know how hard that was for me. But now, God has returned her again to our safe keeping. Be happy, my wife, my dear wife, because you are married to a very happy man! Mona, come out here! I don't care what your mother says!

MOTHER: Yadu'llah. We have a guest.

FATHER: Why do you keep saying that?

MR. ALIZADEH (*entering*): Hello, Yadu'llah.

The FATHER looks at ALIZADEH, then at his wife, and then to MONA, who has entered.

FATHER: I don't think I understand

MONA: Dad, Mr. Alizadeh came to warn us . . .

MR. ALIZADEH: Yadu'llah, you and your family are in danger.

FATHER: We are Baha'is in Iran. We are always in danger.

MR. ALIZADEH: I understand, but we had a close call at the school today. You know I wouldn't have come.

FATHER: Yes. I thank you for your concern.

MONA: Dad. (*Taking him aside.*)

FATHER: Yes, Mona.

MONA: I was just thinking. Dad, listen. I ran into a boy I know. He was with a group of religious men and he told me that we were in danger also.

FATHER: Did he?

MONA: But, Dad, he said tonight.

FATHER: Mona, I appreciate your concern . . .

MONA: Daddy, it's you I'm worried about. I mean they might try to have me expelled from school again, but you . . . you're Secretary of the Shiraz Assembly. They can arrest you, or worse . . .

FATHER: What would you have me do, Mona?

MONA: Maybe we could just go out of town for a couple of days. Dad, maybe this is a message from God or something telling us something that we should be listening to.

FATHER: What if you were in my place, Mona?

MONA: What?

FATHER: If you were the one in danger. It's not unthinkable — you do participate in the Baha'i community. What would you do? Would you leave?

MONA: I . . . I'm not sure. I wasn't thinking about it that way.

MR. ALIZADEH: Miss Mahmudnizhad, it would be a good idea to lay low a little while.

Pause. She looks at her FATHER, *then at* ALIZADEH.

MR. ALIZADEH: What do you say?

A knocking from the balcony.

MRS. KHUDAYAR (*in a loud whisper*): Mahmudnizhad! Mahmudnizhad! (*More knocking.*)

MR. ALIZADEH: Who's that?

FATHER: It's okay. It's our neighbor.

The FATHER *goes to let in* MRS. KHUDAYAR.

FATHER: Welcome. Please come in.

MRS. KHUDAYAR: I just got a call from a friend on the fourth floor. There are several guards in their apartment looking for Baha'is. She thinks they're looking for you, but had the wrong address.

MOTHER: Yadu'llah. What do we do?

MONA (*embracing him*): Daddy, I won't let them take you! I won't!

FATHER (*to* MONA): They can take me nowhere my Beloved has not already been. (*To* ALIZADEH.) My friend, for your own safety, I ask that you leave right away.

MR. ALIZADEH: What about your family? What about your daughter?

FATHER: Mona must make her own decisions.

He goes to the door, opens it and exits.

MR. ALIZADEH: Well?

MONA: How can I leave them?

FATHER (*reentering*): I hear them down the hall. We'll have to find you another way out.

MOTHER: There's the balcony.

FATHER: But that only leads next door.

All look at MRS. KHUDAYAR. *A pounding on the door. Silence.*

MRS. KHUDAYAR: All right, come on, come on. Come with me.

She leads ALIZADEH *out by way of the balcony. He turns before exiting.*

MR. ALIZADEH: She doesn't need to be exposed to this.

FATHER *and daughter look at each other a moment.*

FATHER: You can go.

More pounding, louder.

VOICES (*off*): Hello! Mahmudnizhad! Hey! Anybody home?

MRS. KHUDAYAR: Come on, come on. You'll just be next door.

They exit with MONA. FATHER *and* MOTHER *exchange looks. More pounding. The* FATHER *opens the door. The* MOTHER *runs to fetch a chador (the full body veil). In the hall are* AQA HUSAYNI *and two armed guards. One of the guards turns out to be* ARAM, *who wears a hood partially covering his face.*

FATHER: Good evening, friends. What can I do for you?

GUARD: We are from the Revolutionary Court of Shiraz. We have a warrant to enter your house from the Public Prosecutor.

FATHER: May I see this warrant?

The GUARD *hands him the warrant menacingly. The* FATHER *looks at it.*

FATHER: Please come in.

They enter brusquely. ARAM *looks out of place, a little ashamed.*

AQA HUSAYNI: What's this? Just you two? Aram, check those rooms.

ARAM *exits.*

FATHER: We are the only ones here.

GUARD: Sir, the door to the balcony is open. (*He goes out.*) Sir, the balcony is connected to another apartment.

AQA HUSAYNI: See what you can find.

GUARD *exits.* ARAM *enters, clearly relieved.*

ARAM: All clear, sir.

AQA HUSAYNI: Nobody?

ARAM: No, sir.

AQA HUSAYNI: All right, search these ones for weapons.

MRS. KHUDAYAR: Get out! Get out! Out of my house! Get out!

The GUARD *reenters chased on by* MRS. KHUDAYAR.

MRS. KHUDAYAR: You want to enter my apartment?! You want to accost my guests?! I want to see a warrant! The Baha'is may let you walk all over them, but I won't do it! One call to my brother-in-law and you'll be sorry you ever saw me!

She exits. The GUARD *looks to* AQA HUSAYNI.

AQA HUSAYNI: Let her go. Have these been searched?

ARAM: No, sir.

ARAM *clumsily searches the* MOTHER *and* FATHER. *The other* GUARD *searches the apartment.*

AQA HUSAYNI: Mahmudnizhad, you have two daughters?

FATHER: Yes, sir. One is recently married.

AQA HUSAYNI: You will give me her address.

FATHER: Yes.

MOTHER: Sshh!

FATHER: Farkhundih. We have nothing to hide.

AQA HUSAYNI: That makes our job that much easier. And your other daughter?

FATHER: Yes, sir.

AQA HUSAYNI: Where is she?

FATHER: My other daughter?

AQA HUSAYNI: Yes, I believe my son knows her. What's her name, Aram?

A beat.

ARAM: Mona.

FATHER: Yes, Mona . . . I'm not sure . . . exactly. Perhaps she will be back . . .

The GUARD *enters from the bedroom area and approaches with a photo album, shows* AQA HUSAYNI *a picture.*

AQA HUSAYNI: What is this?

FATHER: These are pictures of my friends.

AQA HUSAYNI: Friends? Do you know who this is?

FATHER: That is Mr. Bakhtavar.

AQA HUSAYNI: Are there others like this?

FATHER: Yes, sir.

AQA HUSAYNI: Come with us. Aram, you stay here and keep watch.

All leave except ARAM. MONA *appears at the patio door. They stare a moment.*

ARAM: You should go. Quickly.

MONA: This is my home.

ARAM: They're in the other room. I won't tell.

MONA: My father is innocent.

ARAM: They want you too.

He shows her the warrant. MONA *takes a deep breath.*

MONA: This is my home.

ARAM: I'll go with you.

MONA: What?

ARAM: I'll get you out of here. Maybe your mother. I'll protect you. I'll leave my father, I will. (*A beat.*) I'll be good to you.

MONA: What about my father?

ARAM *shakes his head.*

MONA: What about my faith?

They look at each other a long moment. ARAM *looks away. The* GUARD *enters, carrying a stack of books. Seeing* MONA *and* ARAM, *he is confused.*

GUARD: Oh. (*He exits.*)

ARAM: They're coming.

MONA: I've made my choice.

The others reenter. The FATHER *sees* MONA.

FATHER: As I've been telling you. We have nothing to hide.

AQA HUSAYNI: Who's this? Your daughter?

FATHER: This is my daughter.

ARAM: Sir, I caught her trying to sneak back in.

> MONA *looks at* ARAM. *He turns away, pulling his hood further on. Silence. The* GUARD *is struggling a little beneath the weight of the books.*

GUARD: What do you want me to do with these?

> AQA HUSAYNI *gestures towards the wedding gift carpet. The* GUARD *drops the books and tries to wrap them in the rug.*

AQA HUSAYNI: We're ready to go. Aram, help him with that rug. (*To* FATHER.) You and the girl. You're coming with us.

FATHER: The girl?

AQA HUSAYNI: Yes. We're bringing you both. Let's go! We're in a hurry.

MOTHER: Mona? You've got to be kidding.

AQA HUSAYNI: No, we're not kidding. Can you get that or what?

GUARD: It's heavy!

MOTHER: If you want to take my husband, okay! But where are you taking this little sixteen-year old girl at this hour of the night?!

AQA HUSAYNI: "This little sixteen-year old"? You should say "this little Baha'i teacher!" The girl is coming with us.

MOTHER: All right. That's it! Take me! Take me instead!

MONA: Mom, calm down.

GUARD: Woman, we don't want you.

MOTHER: Then kill me! Kill me now! KILL ME!! Shoot me right now! (*She grabs the barrel of the* GUARD's *gun.*) There! I'll even aim it for you!

The GUARD *pushes her away.*

GUARD: Crazy woman! Get away! You're crazy!

FATHER: Farkhundih!

MOTHER: What are you going to do? Let them take her?!

FATHER: Farkhundih. (*Looking deeply into the men's faces.*) These men. These men . . . I love these brothers like my own sons. I am sure it is the will of God that they are here now to take Mona and myself away with them. Just leave everything in God's hands and don't worry about Mona. These brothers look on Mona as their own sister.

A beat.

AQA HUSAYNI (*to* GUARD): Will you get that rug? (*To* ARAM.) Help him! Come on! Let's go.

AQA HUSAYNI *exits with the* FATHER. *The men struggle to raise the rug.* MONA *kisses and hugs her* MOTHER.

MONA: Mama, will you be okay?

MOTHER: Oh, Mona . . .

GUARD: I'll get this. Will you get her?

ARAM: Yes.

The GUARD *drags the rug out.* MONA *goes to leave. Her* MOTHER *stops her, removes her own chador, and solemnly helps* MONA *put it on.* MONA *kisses her* MOTHER *and goes to leave. The* MOTHER *rushes out of the room.*

ARAM: Mona?

MONA *stops.*

ARAM: Forgive me.

MONA *goes to leave.*

ARAM: Mona! (*He removes his hood, assuming the character and posture of the* YOUNG MAN *in Mona's dream.*) Forgive me.

MONA *stares amazedly and walks out, speechless. End of scene.*

END OF ACT I

ACT II

Scene I – Prison

The scene begins with MONA *kneeling in the middle of an empty prison cell. She sways a bit, eyes closed, apparently praying. We hear a* WOMAN'S VOICE *offstage as if from an adjoining room.*

WOMAN'S VOICE (*off*): Mona! Where's Mona?

The scene shifts to reveal MR. ALIZADEH's *English classroom.* FARAH *stands before the class, holding a letter, which she prepares to read.*

FARAH: Should I read the whole thing?

MR. ALIZADEH: Please.

FARAH: "Dear Farah, I'm even wondering if you'll get this. We're not supposed to write anything except for filling out all the forms they give us. (I was shocked the first time I saw my file. It was so thick!) But I put my trust in God to get this letter to you — and in Minu who is smuggling it out!" (*A slight pause.*) "I have only seen my father once since coming here. They have done horrible things to him, but he's just become more radiant. Like a candle that's had its cover removed. I don't know if you on the outside can understand. Anyway, I wasn't cooperating, so they brought him in on a cart. His feet were bare so I could see dried blood around his toes. The soles of his feet had been beaten with a rod. The interrogator said that it took several days for the feet to start to bleed but when they did they bled from the nails, and had I ever seen any one's feet bleed? I almost lost it there, but my father said, 'Mona, they hit me and after a

71

while I don't feel the pain any more. Love, Mona. Only love. You must not hate them or be angry with them. Answer them bravely and honestly. We have nothing to hide.' And they took him away." (*A slight pause.*) "Farah, don't worry about me. I have a wonderful family here with my fellow women prisoners, both Baha'is and Muslims. We keep each other up. (The Muslims call me 'little prisoner.') With love, Mona."

> FARAH, *moved, stops reading but remains standing. Again we hear the* WOMAN'S VOICE *from offstage.*

WOMAN'S VOICE (*off*): Mona!

> MONA *opens her eyes.*

MONA: I'll be right in, Zahra.

WOMAN'S VOICE (*off*): Mona, come! Teach me another!

> MONA *resumes her previous position.*

MR. ALIZADEH (*softly*): Is that the end?

FARAH: No. There's a postscript: "Last night, I felt as though I were on a balcony getting closer to the moon. But I kept seeing my mother's face. Farah, please go see her — and my sister — and hug and kiss them for me. They visit, but there's a barrier between us."

> *A pause.* ALIZADEH *is brooding.* MONA *remains still.*

FARAH: That's the end, Mr. Alizadeh.

MR. ALIZADEH: No, Miss Ja'fari. That's not the end.

> *He exits. Lights down on* FARAH *and the class.* MONA *breaks from her meditation. Another prisoner, the* HEAD PRISONER, *has entered quietly from the opposite side and stands by the window.*

HEAD PRISONER: You weren't praying, were you, little prisoner?

MONA: Oh . . . Fakhrí.

HEAD PRISONER: I suppose if you're silent, it can't do any harm.

MONA: Thank you.

HEAD PRISONER: You know he wouldn't have banned them if they didn't work.

WOMAN'S VOICE (*off*): Mona!

MONA *goes to leave.*

HEAD PRISONER: Where are you going?

MONA: Zahra wants to learn another song.

HEAD PRISONER: I've got something for you.

MONA: Oh?

WOMAN'S VOICE (*off*): Mona!!!!

MONA: I'll get it from you later. It sounds like she really needs me. (*She goes to leave.*)

HEAD PRISONER: She's a drug addict in withdrawal — she needs distraction. Little prisoner!

MONA: I'll only be next door.

HEAD PRISONER: Aren't you even curious as to what I have?

MONA: Okay, what is it?

HEAD PRISONER: You'll have to come see.

WOMAN'S VOICE (*off*): Moooonnnnaaaaa!!!

MONA: I'm coming Zahra!! All right then.

She walks over to the HEAD PRISONER, *who hands her a piece of paper.*

MONA (*turning to go*): Thank you.

HEAD PRISONER: Happy Naw-Rúz.

MONA: It's not Naw-Rúz, is it?

The HEAD PRISONER *shakes her head.* MONA *doesn't understand, laughs and exits, unfolding the paper. The* HEAD PRISONER *stares out the window.* MONA *reenters quickly.*

MONA: Is this real?

HEAD PRISONER: Real?

MONA: Yeah, real.

HEAD PRISONER: It's a real release. Whether they let you go is another matter.

MONA: So this means they're letting me go?

HEAD PRISONER: Don't get your hopes too high, little prisoner. They always look for ways to catch you off-guard.

MONA: How will I know?

HEAD PRISONER: If they call you down . . .

MONA: Yeah?

HEAD PRISONER: That'll be a good sign

MONA exits. Shift to another area of the stage, an office in the prison. A MAN *sits in a large chair behind a desk. His back is to*

the audience and his identity is hard to determine. Mona's
MOTHER *enters the office hurriedly.*

MOTHER: I have the money! I have it here in my hand! (*No reaction from the* MAN.) Is this the right room? Excuse me. I was told I was to report here with the security bond for my daughter . . . (*She is handed a piece of paper.*) Oh. (*Another form.*) Okay, but is she, I mean, the time on the paper says now, because it took me a while to come up with the money . . . ? (*No response.*) So I should fill out the forms.

Switch back to the prison cell. MONA *and* ZAHRA, *a frail-looking young woman, reenter.*

ZAHRA: Oh, Mona, this is wonderful! You're going to be free. Where is everyone? Shirin! Roya!

MONA: Most of them are still being questioned. Anyway, Zahra, let's not tell everyone yet.

ZAHRA: So what are you going to do if they release you? Here, sit! Sit!

MONA: I don't know. I haven't had the chance to think.

ZAHRA: What else do we think about in here? I know what I want. The first thing I'm getting when I get out of here is a good meal.

MONA: Yeah?

ZAHRA: Yeah, and I know it's not going to be beans.

MONA: No beans!

ZAHRA: No more beans.

MONA: Never again beans!

ZAHRA: Then there's going to be rice, of course.

MONA: Of course. Rice.

ZAHRA: Rice of course.

MONA: And tadíg?

ZAHRA: Of course.

MONA: Good! I love tadíg!

ZAHRA: And kebab. I love kebab!

HEAD PRISONER: Everyone loves kebab.

MONA: But the way my father makes it!

HEAD PRISONER: So what is it? Chicken or lamb?

ZAHRA: Both. But Mona, they're letting you go! What do you want?

MONA: I don't know. It depends.

ZAHRA: No, Mona. Whatever you want your mother will make you.

MONA: But it depends.

ZAHRA: On what?

MONA: My father. I don't know if he's going to be released.

ZAHRA: Okay, we won't talk about food anymore. Fakhrí! Here, come sit by us. (*The* HEAD PRISONER *doesn't move.*) What about after you eat?

MONA: Oh, Zahra, I don't know. They might not even call me.

ZAHRA: We're not going to talk about that.

MONA: But it's true. And my father, I don't even know . . .

ZAHRA: Don't worry about the kebab.

MONA: I'm not talking about kebab!

ZAHRA: Good. So think about what comes next. Close your eyes. You just ate, what's next?

A long beat.

MONA: A shower.

ZAHRA: A shower!

MONA: A hot shower.

ZAHRA: Oh, yes, a hot shower!

MONA: A long hot shower with soap and a fresh, clean towel to follow.

ZAHRA: Stop, Mona, you're going to make me cry.

MONA: Oh, Zahra, this is sick!

ZAHRA: Keep going, and then?

MONA: Zahra!

ZAHRA: Mona! What do you want?

MONA: What do I want? I want *everyone* to be released. I don't want to be the only one. It's horrible. How can I sleep in my bed when you are all here in the cold?

ZAHRA: We're not going to think about that, Mona.

MONA: I feel torn.

ZAHRA: What do you want?

MONA: Want, want, who cares what I want? No, no, no, Zahra. This is not the way Baha'is think about it. We are here for God! We are in prison for our faith! What I want is what God wants for me! That's what I want. That's what we all want. That's why we're here. That's why when they line us up and give us the choice . . . that's why we always come back here. Because that's what we want. We want what God wants.

Silence.

MONA: It's just hard sometimes to figure out what God actually wants.

Switch back to the prison office.

MOTHER: There you go. Forms all filled out. (*The* MAN *at the desk looks at the forms, then at her, at the forms, and then at her.*) Oh, I would also like to make an inquiry into my husband's condition and arrange a visit. (*She is handed more forms.*) Lot of forms to keep track of, no? (*He doesn't respond, but taps the table.*) Oh, money!

She shuffles through her things.

ZAHRA (*from prison cell*): 500,000 Tuman! That's a lot of money.

The MOTHER *puts the money on the desk. The* MAN *indicates a seat away from his desk. After she sits, he picks up a phone. Switch back to Prison cell. The* HEAD PRISONER *looks out the window.*

HEAD PRISONER: If that doesn't just say it all!

MONA: What?

HEAD PRISONER: That *damn* tree!

ZAHRA: There's no need to curse.

HEAD PRISONER: How about this? That *God-damned* tree!

MONA: What are you talking about?

ZAHRA: So is your mother coming to bail you out?

MONA: I don't know, I don't know! I don't know anything!

ZAHRA: I'm sure she will. She'll find a way. Now you just wait to be called.

HEAD PRISONER (*her volume increasing as she goes*): God-damned fruit falling off a God-damned tree on the God-damned lawn of this God-damned prison in this God-forsaken country! (*Pause while the other women look at her.*) We are dying of scurvy in here and there are plums rotting on the ground out there!

ZAHRA: What are you talking about?

HEAD PRISONER: The Iranian people are kept in poverty while the oil-rich bastard traitors and their English friends make millions!

She leaves. A beat. She reenters. A beat. ZAHRA *has begun to tremble.*

ZAHRA: Do you ever want to get married, Mona?

MONA: Why is everyone always asking me about that?

ZAHRA: Don't you want to get married?

MONA: Of course I do. I mean, I don't know. I'm in a prison with all women, Zahra. I just want to know if my mother and father are okay.

HEAD PRISONER: Marriage is oppression. You're better off in prison.

Pause.

MONA: They haven't called yet, have they.

A phone rings in the prison office. Mona's MOTHER *anxiously awaits some news.*

MAN BEHIND DESK *(answering)*: Mm-hmm . . . Mm-hmm . . . Mm-hmm. *(He hangs up.)*

Switch back to prison cell. All the women sit slumped up together. ZAHRA *rocks and shivers between* MONA *and the* HEAD PRISONER, *who try to comfort her.*

HEAD PRISONER: If I had a choice? First. Definitely. Get it over with.

MONA: I don't know. Maybe. Definitely not last. That's too much.

ZAHRA: What? What are you two . . . ? You're not dying! You're not! You're not . . .

Switch to prison office.

MOTHER: What? What is it?

MAN *(standing)*: Mrs. Mahmudnizhad?

MOTHER: Yes.

MAN: That's your name?

MOTHER: Yes.

MAN: Farkhundih Mahmudnizhad?

MOTHER: Yes.

The MAN *walks behind her. We now see it is the* RELIGIOUS MAGISTRATE *from Scene Four.*

MAGISTRATE: Well, Mrs. Farkhundih Mahmudnizhad. I have some good news and I have some bad news. The bad news is: It seems there's a warrant out for your arrest.

MOTHER: My arrest?

MAGISTRATE: Yes, for involvement in prohibited religious activities.

MOTHER: But what about . . .

MAGISTRATE: The good news? The good news is your bail has been set at 500,000 Tuman. You're free to leave.

He pulls out the money from the envelope, fans it and smiles. MONA *slowly tears her release in half. The voice of her* FATHER *is heard.*

FATHER: YAAAAAHHHHHH!

The FATHER *is revealed. He sits upright with his feet extended forward.*

FATHER: I don't . . . don't . . . under . . . under . . . stand . . . I, I, I don't . . . why you . . . you . . . yoooouuu.

MONA *tears the paper again. A loud crack.*

FATHER: YAAAAAAAAAAHHHHH!!! I've told, told you, you, you . . . . the . . . the . . . truuuuuuth.

MONA *continues tearing. Another loud crack.*

FATHER: YAAAAAAAAAHHHHHH!!! O Baha'u'llah! Thank you! Thank you! (*He starts to laugh.*) I see!! Yes.

Another crack.

FATHER: OOOOOOOOHHHHHH!!! Ya Baha'u-l'abha!! Give these men all that they desire! Give them all good things!

A louder crack.

FATHER: AAAAAAAAAAHHHHHH!!! (*Lower.*) Thank you. Thank you. Thank you.

MONA *drops the torn pieces like snow. Lights fade on the* FATHER. *Mona's* MOTHER *slowly stands. She turns to go, but then turns back.*

MOTHER: O God, I want my child. I want Mona from you. I want to touch her, to kiss her cheek. I want my baby. The little birds are all flying free but my little bird is trapped in a cage.

Fade on MOTHER. *An announcement comes over the Intercom. It is the voice of* AQA HUSAYNI. *Immediately, the women are expectant.*

AQA HUSAYNI: Attention prisoners. Attention. The Religious Magistrate has ordered that Baha'i prisoners are no longer to associate with Muslim prisoners. Muslim prisoners are no longer to associate with Baha'i prisoners. Effective immediately. Head prisoners in each cell are required to enforce this order . . . That is all.

A moment where the women, leaning on one another, absorb this. The HEAD PRISONER *rises first, and pulls the trembling* ZAHRA *away from* MONA. *Silence.*

MONA: Fakhrí, wait. I want to see.

A beat.

HEAD PRISONER: But you said you didn't.

MONA: I think I'm ready now.

> *The* HEAD PRISONER *digs in her pocket and pulls out a small mirror case.* MONA *opens it and looks into it. She closes it and hands it back to the* HEAD PRISONER, *who exits with* ZAHRA. MONA *is left alone. End of scene.*

Scene 2 – An Interrogation Room

AQA HUSAYNI *enters, followed by* MR. ALIZADEH.

AQA HUSAYNI: This room is not being used. It will be a short wait.

The AQA *exits.* MR. ALIZADEH *takes a moment to look around, then sits.* MONA *enters.*

MONA (*surprised*): Oh . . .

MR. ALIZADEH: Miss Mahmudnizhad.

MONA: Mister Alizadeh, Hi! What . . . ?

MR. ALIZADEH: It's good to see you again.

MONA: It's good to see you! What are you doing here? I . . . I wasn't . . . This isn't how we normally meet with visitors.

MR. ALIZADEH: Miss Mahmudnizhad. I've come to bring you home.

MONA (*amazed*): What? How? I didn't bring my things. I didn't say goodbye. Can I — (*She screams.*) But when can we? I mean — why are you smiling like that? Is this a joke?

MR. ALIZADEH: It's good to see you so happy.

MONA: I probably look silly. Mr. Alizadeh, what happened? I mean, it was supposed to be a while ago. Not that I'm complaining!

MR. ALIZADEH: You've been here far too long.

MONA: But why is it you? I suppose I thought my mother would come. Is she all right? Do you know?

MR. ALIZADEH: I'm sure she's fine.

MONA: What did you do? It's hard for me to believe . . . O God!!

MR. ALIZADEH: What is it?

MONA: I tore up the release. (*Pause.*) I did. I tore it up. It's in pieces on the floor. The release form.

MR. ALIZADEH: Release form?

MONA: Yes, you need it to get through the gate. Oh, no.

MR. ALIZADEH: I'm sure we can work that out.

MONA: Do you have a copy? Maybe I can use that.

MR. ALIZADEH: I don't . . . I . . .

MONA: You . . . ?

MR. ALIZADEH: I was not aware there was a release form.

MONA: Oh . . . Well, I just got it today.

MR. ALIZADEH: Oh?

MONA: My mother was to come bail me out.

MR. ALIZADEH: Really?

MONA: That was supposed to be hours ago.

MR. ALIZADEH: Oh.

MONA: You didn't know about that?

MR. ALIZADEH: No.

MONA: Then how did you know?

MR. ALIZADEH: I hadn't heard of the release.

MONA: Oh.

MR. ALIZADEH: Not that it wouldn't be welcome news.

MONA: But, Mr. Alizadeh, why would you be here if you hadn't heard about the release? You said you'd come to bring me home.

MR. ALIZADEH: This has gone on too long, Miss Mahmud-nizhad. You don't know how happy I am to see you so energetic, still so full of life. I was afraid I detected a hint of resignation in your letter to Miss Ja'fari.

MONA: The letter? Farah got the letter?

MR. ALIZADEH: Yes, she got it, and she read it before the whole class. I must say, we were very moved . . .

MONA: Oh.

MR. ALIZADEH: Very moved.

MONA: So wait . . . That's why you're here? The letter?

MR. ALIZADEH: Hearing your words set me on fire. I had to come. I had no other choice.

MONA: But what about the release?

MR. ALIZADEH: Miss Mahmudnizhad. I just spoke to the authorities here. There was no mention of your release.

MONA: You said you'd come to bring me home. What did you mean?

MR. ALIZADEH: Miss Mahmudnizhad, I am here to discuss with you your options.

MONA: My options?

MR. ALIZADEH: Yes.

MONA: So I'm not free.

MR. ALIZADEH: Well, not yet . . . no. But I tell you, your vigor for freedom is very promising. After all, it really is within your power to negotiate your freedom.

MONA: Mr. Alizadeh, I don't know if you know this but the only way they'll release us is if we claim to not be Baha'is.

MR. ALIZADEH (*gravely*): Yes.

MONA: So I really don't have any other options.

MR. ALIZADEH: Miss Mahmudnizhad, I am ashamed. I am ashamed to find you here. I am ashamed that Iran has fallen so low that it casts its innocent children into prison.

MONA: You don't have to be ashamed. I'm not.

MR. ALIZADEH: You should be free! You should be in school, learning! How can they do this? It was one thing to hear about it, but now to see you . . . No, I cannot allow this.

MONA: Mr. Alizadeh. I'm in prison because of my beliefs. There is no shame in that.

MR. ALIZADEH: No this is unacceptable!

MONA: I appreciate that, Mr. Alizadeh. I do. But there's nothing you can do. We have to leave this in God's hands.

MR. ALIZADEH: Is that how you really feel?

MONA: Yes. I'm content.

MR. ALIZADEH: Really?

MONA: Really. There's nothing you can do.

MR. ALIZADEH: Nothing? Before I was brought to this room, Aqa Husayni told me there were several women here in prison that were about to be convicted of capital crimes. I asked if my student was one of them. He said, yes. And then he asked me — *me* — to help him.

MONA: To do what? Convince me to recant?

MR. ALIZADEH: Clarify your options.

MONA: Mr. Alizadeh, I'm grateful that you've come to see me. I am. But if you've only come to convince me to renounce my religion . . .

MR. ALIZADEH: Are you afraid I might succeed?

MONA: I'm afraid of nothing.

MR. ALIZADEH: Nothing? Nothing, Mahmudnizhad? What if they torture you? What if they torture someone you love? You're not the only one you have to think about.

MONA: Mr. Alizadeh . . .

MR. ALIZADEH: Are you afraid of truth, Mahmudnizhad?

Pause.

MONA: No. I'm not.

MR. ALIZADEH: Then you can listen to this old bachelor foreign-language teacher whose only wish is to see his students grow and flourish?

MONA: Of course.

MR. ALIZADEH: Thank you. (*A beat.*) You know, you're just like him.

MONA: What?

MR. ALIZADEH: Your father. You have your father's faith.

MONA: I follow the same religion as my father, Mr. Alizadeh. My faith is my own.

MR. ALIZADEH: Miss Mahmudnizhad, I am not here to convert you. I'm only here to talk to you about your options. I do not like the clergy. But, Miss Mahmudnizhad, I can find nothing of any worth in you dying for a belief.

MONA: I understand why you might feel that way, but you are not a Baha'i.

MR. ALIZADEH: I know something about your religion, Miss Mahmudnizhad.

MONA: You are a Muslim, Mister Alizadeh?

MR. ALIZADEH: I was born a Muslim.

MONA: Did Imam Husayn do well in dying for his faith?

MR. ALIZADEH: My dear, you are not Imam Husayn. Mourners will not pour onto the streets for you. They will not put up a wailing every year to remember your sacrifice. Too many people have already died for causes. We don't have room for you on our calendar.

MONA: I'm not doing this to be remembered by your calendar. I'm doing this for God.

MR. ALIZADEH: Yes, I know. I know something about your religion. Some very good people, and they say some good things about education . . .

MONA: Men and women.

MR. ALIZADEH: Most admirable. But, Miss Mahmudnizhad, the goal of education is to make this a better world, and yet you seem all too ready to give it all up for some other world. Doesn't this seem to be a contradiction?

MONA: No, it's . . .

MR. ALIZADEH: It sounds like fundamentalism.

MONA: Am I killing myself? If it were up to me, I'd be back in school . . .

MR. ALIZADEH: But it is up to you!

MONA: How?

MR. ALIZADEH: Just tell them what they want to hear and you're free to go.

MONA: Mr. Alizadeh, you care about truth?

MR. ALIZADEH: Truth? What is truth? The truth is uncertain. Even within Islam, there are different opinions about what truth is.

MONA: You stood up for me when the clergy was trying to empty the school of Baha'is.

MR. ALIZADEH: Yes.

MONA: Why did you do that?

MR. ALIZADEH: Because I wanted to see you thrive and flourish, and *live*.

MONA: Wouldn't it have just been easier to allow them to expel me?

MR. ALIZADEH: Easier? . . . No. I couldn't have lived with myself.

MONA: Exactly. And I couldn't live with myself if I were to recant.

MR. ALIZADEH: But there is a difference between me putting up with some heat from the clergy and you throwing away your life.

MONA: How do you know they can't burn your house down?

MR. ALIZADEH: I live in an apartment.

MONA: No free thinker is safe in this society, Mr. Alizadeh. Didn't you say that?

MR. ALIZADEH: That doesn't mean we throw ourselves into the fire.

MONA: Do you think you're the only one who should sacrifice?

MR. ALIZADEH: That's absurd. I love what I do. I have sacrificed nothing.

MONA: So if I told you I love my Faith more than anything else?

MR. ALIZADEH: I'd say you're a fool to throw away your life for words.

MONA: Words?

MR. ALIZADEH: Words! That's all they are! Like words in a book. Close the book and they are gone!

MONA: This book is my life, Mr. Alizadeh!

MR. ALIZADEH: Precisely. (*A beat.*) Your faith advocates moderation in all things.

MONA: It also demands absolute truthfulness.

MR. ALIZADEH: And yet 'Abdu'l-Baha said you could lie to a dying man if it would comfort his mind. How do you explain that contradiction?

MONA: 'Abdu'l-Baha said that?

MR. ALIZADEH: I know something about your Faith, Miss Mahmudnizhad.

MONA: Where did he say that?

MR. ALIZADEH: *Some Answered Questions.* Chapter 57. Verse 12.

MONA: I need to check that. But even then, that doesn't mean I shouldn't tell the truth about my belief.

MR. ALIZADEH: What is the truth, Miss Mahmudnizhad? Show me an absolute statement about any subject in your writings, and I will show you another to contradict it.

MONA: I don't believe you.

MR. ALIZADEH: Try me.

MONA: I don't believe you.

MR. ALIZADEH: I'll prove it to you. Try me.

MONA: Okay, in the Baha'i writings it says that we should investigate the truth for ourselves and that we should ask questions.

MR. ALIZADEH: Baha'u'llah: "The most burning fire is to question the signs of God." *Words of Wisdom.* Verse 18.

MONA: I don't see that as . . .

MR. ALIZADEH: I know something about your faith.

MONA: But . . .

MR. ALIZADEH: There are no absolutes.

MONA: Why are you saying this?

MR. ALIZADEH: Because you are my student.

MONA: Baha'is don't dissemble their faith.

MR. ALIZADEH: Baha'u'llah says that Baha'is should act with wisdom to avoid persecutions.

MONA: Baha'is don't dis-

MR. ALIZADEH: But what about you, Mona? What about Mona? What does Mona think about it? Investigate the truth for yourself. You say you're not afraid, but maybe you're just a little afraid to think for yourself?

MONA: No.

MR. ALIZADEH: Not even a little? (*Pause.*) You had a dream that you told me about. With the dresses.

 MONA *looks down.*

MR. ALIZADEH: You chose the blue one if I recall correctly . . . but that doesn't seem right. The blue one was about life and service if I remember correctly . . . Am I wrong? You did believe that dream to contain a message, did you not? Mona?

MONA: Yes.

MR. ALIZADEH: So who was this message from? From God? Because God also appears to be the one telling you to die for your faith. Well, which is it? Life or death? Or maybe God is confused?

MONA: How dare you say that?!

MR. ALIZADEH: It was a question. Am I not allowed to ask questions?

MONA: God is not confused. You may be. I may be. God is not confused.

MR. ALIZADEH: But, you see, I don't think it was God sending you that dream. I think it was your own unconscious. Maybe it sensed that your life was in danger, so it fashioned a creative way of telling you . . .

MONA: No. It was more that that.

MR. ALIZADEH: The other option is a confused God. Are you ready to die for a confused God?

MONA: Why are you doing this? I don't know why you're doing this.

MR. ALIZADEH: You are my student . . .

MONA (*a discovery*): You were a Baha'i.

A beat.

MR. ALIZADEH: I was.

MONA: What happened?

MR. ALIZADEH: I woke up.

A beat.

MONA: Do you believe in God, Mr. Alizadeh?

MR. ALIZADEH: I cannot believe in a God at war with Himself.

MONA: I'll be honest with you. I didn't expect to face this situation. I didn't. But I have not been abandoned. I'm seeing things now . . . Life and death. They don't mean the same things any more. Everything around us is telling us how fleeting this life is. But God is present with us in this very moment, Mr. Alizadeh. Do you feel Him? He doesn't speak through human language, Mr. Alizadeh. He speaks in the heart. And sometimes it takes time to understand what He's saying.

MR. ALIZADEH (*harshly*): What you're really talking about is another father figure that you can cling to when your real father is dead.

MONA: I am not clinging to my father.

MR. ALIZADEH: Then listen to what I'm saying and stand on your own!

MONA (*standing, trembling*): I stand on my own. I have left the house of my father. My clothes are packed. My rugs rolled up. And I'm on a journey. To the abode of my lover.

MR. ALIZADEH: Your . . .

MONA: I am a bride. And this is my wedding day. This is my wedding dress. The dress I have chosen. The dress I have put on. And no one will take it off me . . . until my wedding night. And then only him.

MR. ALIZADEH: What if someone kills him first?

MONA: What?

MR. ALIZADEH: Your lover.

MONA: What are you . . . ?

MR. ALIZADEH (*gesturing*): What if someone holds him in front of you and — with a word — slits his throat? Because I can do that. With a word. I can kill with a word. (*A beat.*) Dead. He's dead. Your lover is dead. And you are alone in this world.

A beat.

MONA: Mr. Alizadeh, I just saw someone die.

MR. ALIZADEH: Yes.

MONA: Mr. Alizadeh, it was you.

End of scene.

Scene 3 – The Site of the House of the Báb

FARAH *sits. Her shoes are off. She sits a moment, wrestling with her grief.* ARAM *enters, alone, but dressed in his religious attire. He sees* FARAH, *hesitates, then approaches her.*

FARAH: Mr. Alizadeh said they're not going to let her out.

ARAM: I heard.

A beat.

FARAH: Are you just going to stand there?

He comes forward to sit down.

FARAH: Take off your shoes.

ARAM: Why?

FARAH: Because Mona did.

He considers a moment, then takes off his shoes and sits.

FARAH: Where have you been? I haven't seen you much.

ARAM: I've been around. I see you . . . not seeing me.

A beat.

FARAH: I'm not used to you wearing that.

ARAM: It doesn't really fit me.

A beat. FARAH *begins to cry.*

ARAM: I'm sorry.

FARAH *cries harder.*

ARAM: Farah, I'm sorry.

FARAH (*trying to stop, failing, wiping her nose*): Do you have a handkerchief or something?

ARAM (*checking his pockets*): Oh . . . No, I guess I don't.

FARAH (*crying more, and trying to wipe her nose with her hands*): Ugghh! It won't stop. You don't have anything? My nose won't stop running. Mona! You jerk! Look what you're doing to me! I came to your favorite place to remember you and now look at me!

ARAM: She can't hear you.

FARAH (*turning on him, sharply*): What?

ARAM: She's not dead . . .

FARAH: Why did you say that?

ARAM: It's true.

FARAH: Why did you have to say that? You think I can't read your mind. Why don't you just say what you mean? Yet! She's not dead yet!

ARAM: That's not what I meant. You have um . . . (*Indicating her nose.*)

FARAH: I know! So why are you looking at me? Leave me a little dignity, will you? Why don't you just leave?

ARAM: I feel responsible.

FARAH: Go away! You're only responsible for making me feel stupider than I already do.

ARAM: Here. (*He takes off his turban and offers it to her.*)

FARAH: What?

ARAM: Use this.

FARAH: I can't take that. It's religious.

ARAM: It can be washed.

FARAH: Listen! I'd rather stand here dripping head to toe with tears and snot for the rest of the night than go to hell because I defiled that thing!

ARAM (*moving towards her*): We won't let you go to hell.

FARAH: Aram!

ARAM: Be still!

> *He grabs her and wipes her face and hands with equal measure of force and gentleness. She is still while he does it. When he finishes she glares at him. He can't help but crack a smile.*

FARAH: You touched me.

ARAM: Yes.

FARAH: You're gonna pay for that.

ARAM: You're not unclean.

FARAH: Completely covered with mucous.

ARAM: Mucous is okay. Where would we be without mucous?

FARAH: Maybe I'm a Baha'i.

ARAM: Maybe.

FARAH: You touched me.

ARAM: I did.

FARAH: It's gonna cost you.

> FARAH *looks away. They both restrain smiles. End of scene.*

Scene 4 – Prison

Prisoners Visitation Room. A desk and chairs with a glass barrier separating the prisoners' side from the visitors'. There are phone receivers on either side. A GUARD ushers Mona's MOTHER to the seat, indicates the receiver, and then leaves. The MOTHER waits anxiously. After a moment, MONA enters. She is bundled up with clothing.

MONA: Oh, Mama. Hi. Hi.

She sits down and waves to her, picking up the phone receiver. The MOTHER picks up as well. Throughout the conversation we can only hear MONA's voice.

MONA: Hi Mama. Hi . . . I know it's really good to see you too . . . I'm fine. It's just a cold . . . Yeah, three times a day. How are *you* doing? . . . Worried about what? . . . Like what? . . . Mama, please don't say that. (MONA *wipes her nose with her sleeve.*) It's just, It's just really good to see you . . . I don't know, I haven't really thought about it . . . I'm sorry, I'm just . . . I don't know how it looks to you out there, but from where I'm sitting . . . Don't be upset. I don't want you to be upset. (*She sighs.*) You're right. It's possible. I'm just tired. My body's tired. My mind's tired. (*A beat.*) Mom, I need to ask you something. Don't get upset . . . If they do execute me . . . That's not what I have to say. Will you let me ask? . . . Don't cry, Mama. It's really not sad, really . . . But if it *does*. If God wants to take me . . . But Mama, it's a great honor. (*She shudders.*) No, it's just . . . I know I'm not God, but you have to accept that it may happen! And if it does, what

will you do? . . . Mom, but if it does, what will you do? . . . Mom,
I need to . . . Mama, please listen to me. Please. This is important . . . . Are you listening? . . . I need to know that you'll be
safe . . . Safe is that you'll have food to eat, a place to sleep . . .
Mom, don't say that. You have to care . . . Please don't say that.
You do still have a reason. Please. Please don't . . . Please don't
put that on me. I have enough.

> MONA *looks away from her* MOTHER. *The door opens. The*
> FATHER *enters, walking slowly and with difficulty.*

GUARD: Three minutes, Mahmudnizhad.

MONA: Daddy! (*She goes to him.*)

FATHER: Hello, my darling daughter. (*They embrace. He takes her
face in his hands and smiles.*) Is that your mother's voice I heard
all the way down the hall?

MONA: Mom's here. How are you? Are you okay?

FATHER: It's nothing. Hello Farkhundih, it will take me a
minute to get over there, my dear.

MONA: She can't hear you, Dad. Let me help.

FATHER: Thank you. (*Picking up the phone.*) Hello, my dear
one . . . No, no, it's nothing. I'm a little stiff . . . Free? You
think you're free? You on the outside are in the harsher prison! . . . No, I'm lucky. I have my own room . . .

> *He squeezes* MONA's *hand and smiles. She looks down.*

FATHER: One minute, my dear. (*He puts the phone to his chest.*)
Mona, there's something in your heart.

> MOTHER *talks animatedly pointing at* MONA.

MONA: It's nothing, Dad. Talk to Mom. She wants to talk to
you.

FATHER: Do you want to share it?

MONA: What do you want me to say?

FATHER: Only what you want.

A long beat. The MOTHER *bangs on the window. The* FATHER *puts his hand up to the glass where hers is and holds it there, but keeps his eyes on* MONA.

MONA: Mr. Alizadeh came to see me.

FATHER: He did.

MONA: Yes, and he said all these things. I don't know why he would do what he did, but with that and everything else, my head is buzzing, and . . .

FATHER: It's okay.

MONA: I just have all these questions now.

FATHER: Questions?

MONA: I have these times of clarity, of peace — But then there are moments where I forget and I have to call out to God to get me back, to remind me. And it comes, it does. But it's that place in between, Dad, it's that place in between. That's the most dangerous place. What if they get me when I'm there? Sometimes they keep us standing so long, I start to sleep standing up. (*A beat.*) I'm afraid. (*Pause.*) I'm afraid of what happens next. I'm afraid they'll come for me when I'm not ready. I'm afraid for Mom. I'm afraid for you. Dad, I don't know . . . I don't know . . . I'm afraid. I'm afraid. I feel like I'm being ripped up by the roots. I just don't want to mess this up. This is everything.

A beat.

FATHER (*raising the phone*): Farkhundih, you will help me? Good — Mona, your teacher *was* a Baha'i and an active one. He was an exceptional scholar — Yes, Farkhundih — and speaker as well. All of the girls were in love with him. Actually, before we were married, I think your mother . . . — Excuse me, Farkhundih, you don't need to shout, I hear you just fine, my dear. — Mona, are you blushing?

MONA (*trying to cover up a blush*): What? So, what happened?

FATHER: At a certain point, he began to cause problems in the community.

MONA: Like what?

FATHER: Disunity. He began to question the institutions, the teachings themselves.

MONA: And?

FATHER: He left the Faith voluntarily.

MONA: Oh.

FATHER: He was a good man. He was a good friend to me. For a long time.

MONA: Then what happened? I mean, why did he do it? Why would anyone do that?

FATHER: Farkhundih, hold on — Your mother is listing the reasons. (*He laughs.*) — I'm sorry, my dear, but I'm not going to repeat these things you're saying — Mona, you've seen him with your own eyes. You know his qualities. Perhaps you can unravel the mystery yourself.

A beat. MONA *nods, looking down.*

FATHER: The way I understand it, the wisdom of the martyrs is that they never know, they can never be sure — but somehow they persevere. And some, in that final moment, unravel the meaning of love.

Silence. MONA *looks at her* MOTHER. *She kisses her hand and puts it to the glass where her* MOTHER *puts her hand. She takes her* FATHER's *hand, leans forward, kissing him on the cheek. They sit holding each other's hand as best they can. A moment of silence.*

GUARD: Time's up, Mahmudnizhad.

The sound of a prison door slamming shut. The lights go off except for a single harsh light center stage. MONA *comes forward to stand in the light. As she comes into it, she is overtaken by exhaustion.*

MONA: How much longer are you going to keep me here? My legs are numb. (*Her head falls. She starts.*) No! Gotta stay . . . here. Okay. (*She struggles to open her eyes.*) What did you want? (*She struggles.*) I am still . . . I am still awake! (*Her head falls.*) Awake. (*She walks around in a small circle, stomping, trying to stay conscious.*) I'm awake!

She falls asleep, standing. Pounding is heard. Slow pulses of red light come up on Mona's MOTHER, *who sits as before. She pounds on the glass barrier.*

MOTHER: Mona, wake up!

MONA (*rousing*): I am!

Mona's FATHER *rises from where he was seated and walks past* MONA.

FATHER: Love, Mona. Only love.

MONA: Dad.

FATHER: These hours of separation will pass in no time.

MONA: Dad, how did you do it?

FATHER: Before you realize it we will all be together again.

MONA: They're trying to break me. They want to destroy me.

More pounding from MOTHER.

MONA: Mama, let go.

FATHER: Would you like me to turn the light off for you?

MONA: How did you look at them, look into their eyes and smile? You called them your brothers.

FATHER: May my life be sacrificed for you, my love.

MONA: How can you love the one who would destroy you?

Silence. The FATHER *disappears. Lights on* MOTHER *fade. Three* HOODED FIGURES *emerge. One of the* FIGURES *speaks. It's the voice of the* YOUNG MAN *from Mona's earlier vision.*

YOUNG MAN: Look for me.

MONA turns. The FIRST FIGURE *pulls out a blue dress.* MONA *goes to the* FIRST FIGURE *and looks beneath the hood, shakes her head "no", then moves to the* SECOND FIGURE, *who has pulled out a black dress.* MONA *looks under the* SECOND FIGURE's *hood and again shakes her head. These two* FIGURES *exit. The* THIRD FIGURE *stands still, holding a box with a red ribbon.* MONA *removes his hood to reveal the* YOUNG MAN.

MONA: It's you. The dress is different.

YOUNG MAN: I am there when you look for me.

MONA: I've seen you.

YOUNG MAN: In the face of others—

MONA: Yes.

YOUNG MAN: Look for me.

MONA: Who are you?

From the side, we hear AQA HUSAYNI.

AQA HUSAYNI: Mahmudnizhad!

YOUNG MAN: I am . . . . (*He points at her.*)

GUARD: Mona Mahmudnizhad! Stand up!

The scene shifts. The AQA *is present. As* MONA *comes to, her bodily exhaustion returns. The* YOUNG MAN *moves to a corner of the stage and begins to change costume. Gradually,* MONA *becomes aware that she is in an interrogation room, but the* YOUNG MAN *remains in view.* MONA *checks her eyes, trying to differentiate the two worlds.* AQA HUSAYNI *gets up, ready for business. He is unaware of the presence of the* YOUNG MAN.

AQA HUSAYNI: Are you ready to give up this charade?

MONA: Charade?

AQA HUSAYNI: This little game you're playing here?

MONA: I don't know what you mean.

AQA HUSAYNI: This life of lies and deceit. This world of dreams and shadow-play.

MONA: Your honor, I . . .

AQA HUSAYNI: What? "I — what"? Say it. You can say it.

The YOUNG MAN *turns around and looks at* MONA. *He has been putting on a religious cleric's costume.*

MONA: I don't know what to say.

AQA HUSAYNI & YOUNG MAN: Shall I make it plain for you?

MONA (*to the* YOUNG MAN): Please.

> *The* YOUNG MAN *bows his head to* MONA, *slips on his hood and exits.*

AQA HUSAYNI: Very well. Your parents have deceived and mis-led you. They have forced you to imitate them in following the Baha'i religion.

MONA (*not what she was expecting to hear*): What?

AQA HUSAYNI: I said your parents have deceived and mis . . .

MONA: Your honor, I heard what you said.

AQA HUSAYNI: Then why did you ask?

MONA: It's just . . . It's true, your honor, that I was born into a Baha'i family, but I have made up my own mind to be a Baha'i.

AQA HUSAYNI: Young girl, what do you know about religion?

MONA: What more proof of my faith do you want? Here I am in front of you!

AQA HUSAYNI: What harm did you find in Islam that made you turn away from it?

MONA: I believe in Islam, your honor. But I also believe that God has sent a new Messenger, Baha'u'llah, and He has brought new laws . . .

AQA HUSAYNI: Muhammad is the Seal of the Prophets! There will be no more Messengers!

MONA (*overlapping*): Now if by Islam you mean the hatred and bloodshed going on in this country, now that is the reason I'm a Baha'i!

AQA HUSAYNI: Silence!

The RELIGIOUS MAGISTRATE *has entered.*

MAGISTRATE: Aqa Husayni.

AQA HUSAYNI: Magistrate! Forgive me, I was not aware of your presence.

MAGISTRATE: I will take over from here.

AQA HUSAYNI: Yes, your honor.

The AQA *exits. The* MAGISTRATE *holds Mona's file.*

MAGISTRATE: So . . . Miss Mahmudnizhad.

MONA: Yes, sir.

MAGISTRATE: Is there anything I can do to make you more comfortable?

She doesn't respond.

MAGISTRATE: Chair to sit on? (*He fetches her a chair.*) Piece of fruit? (*He pulls an orange from his pocket and sets it before her.*)

MONA: Thank you, sir. (*She keeps her gaze lowered.*)

MAGISTRATE: I came across an interesting thing. Under "desired profession," you have "service to humanity." It's a noble thing, Mona. May I call you Mona?

MONA: Yes, sir.

MAGISTRATE: Truly. A very noble thing.

MONA (*very softly*): Thank you.

MAGISTRATE: You also have here that one of your role models in this respect is your father.

MONA: Yes, sir.

MAGISTRATE: He must be very proud. Your father has been of great service to us here. Reminding the Baha'is that they have nothing to hide. What about you, Mona? Do you have something to hide?

MONA: No, sir.

MAGISTRATE: No doubts or fears, stray thoughts, questions why you're really here? (*A beat.*) Mona?

MONA: I have nothing to hide, your honor.

MAGISTRATE: Then tell me why you're here.

MONA: I served as a teacher for a Baha'i children's class.

A beat.

MAGISTRATE: Would you like to see him? Your father?

She looks up at him.

MAGISTRATE: Yes? (*To a* GUARD.) Go ahead, bring him in. (*To* MONA.) Yes, go. Go to him, my dear.

The doors open and the FATHER *is wheeled in on a gurney, seated upright.* MONA *goes to embrace him, then jumps back.*

MONA: Wha?!

MAGISTRATE (*laughing*): What's wrong? Daddy seem a little cold?

MONA: Oh, Daddy! What have they . . . ? (*A beat. Softly.*) Good for you. Good for you. (*She kisses him and begins to cry.*)

MAGISTRATE: Is this what you want for you, girl?

She doesn't respond. The FATHER's *body is wheeled out.*

MAGISTRATE: That is what you want?! That?! That cold lump of flesh there?! That is 'service', Mona?! Get up! (*He kicks away her chair.*) Give me light! (*Lights come on.*) When God's revolution came to this country, we took away your ability to congregate. We dissolved your institutions. We closed the border to keep you from spreading. What is happening to your potential for service? We denied you rights of citizenship. We had you expelled from schools, fired from your jobs. Your homes were burnt, your leaders executed, your holy places destroyed. Do you see what is happening to your service? You come here, cut off from the world, you have nothing, you are completely at our disposal. Well then, you think, you can help the others in the cell with you. Now you can't go near them. You wanted to pray. I took the words right out of your mouth. (*A beat.*) Now you feel that breath surging in and out of your nostrils, Mona? Huh? You feel that hot, moist breath surging in and out? Mona, I can take that away too. How are you going to serve then, Mona, when Mona is no more?

MONA *doesn't respond.*

MAGISTRATE: What do you say to that, my child?

MONA: Then somehow, I will serve . . . in death.

MAGISTRATE: Serve whom, Mona? Do you think anyone will ever remember what happens to you here? (*A beat.*) Do you think this is cruel? Do you? Can you forgive me? I love this country. I love Iran. And I love all the people in it, though I send every last one to the grave! I love them the way God loves them. With justice. And justice, in our sight, is only mercy. Do you feel my love for you, Mona? I am your real father, Mona. I am telling you the truth, Mona. So will you forgive me? Mona?

MONA: There's nothing to forgive. (*A beat.*) You lead me to my Beloved.

MAGISTRATE: We must obey the Qur'an. Accept Islam or face execution.

MONA: I kiss the order of execution.

> *Lighting change.* MONA *begins to shake. The* MAGISTRATE *comes forward and takes her hands. As he speaks, we hear also the voice of Mona's* FATHER.

MAGISTRATE & FATHER: I am entertaining last requests. What do you want?

MONA: Perseverance.

> *The* FATHER *enters, looking as he did at the beginning of the play.*

MAGISTRATE & FATHER: What do you want from me?

MONA: Perseverance for all the Baha'is.

MAGISTRATE & FATHER: Mona, what do you want for yourself from me?

MONA: Perseverance.

FATHER: It is granted.

> MONA *kisses the hand of the* MAGISTRATE. *She then looks into his face. She lifts her hands and removes his turban, his beard*

and his glasses to reveal the YOUNG MAN *from her earlier visions. His outer garment falls to the ground. He smiles as she stares at him. After a moment, he moves behind her.*

YOUNG MAN (*gently*): Are you ready?

MONA *nods. A noose is revealed.* MONA *takes a step towards it.*

MONA: Wait. (*A beat.*) Last. I want to be last.

YOUNG MAN: Are you afraid?

MONA: No. I want to pray for the others.

YOUNG MAN: It is granted.

MONA *lowers her head in silent prayer as the* FATHER *begins to read off the names of the Ten Women Martyrs of Shiraz. A carpet is spread before the noose, and as the names are read, people come out carrying, with great care, dresses representing each woman.*

FATHER (*throughout*): Shírín Dálvand. Táhirih Síyávushí. Roya Ishráqí. 'Izzat Ishráqí. Zarrín Muqímí. Símín Sábirí. Nusrat Yaldá'í. Mahshíd Nírúmand. Akhtar Sabet. Mona Mahmúd-nizhád.

When MONA *is called, she and the* YOUNG MAN *together remove her chador, revealing the red dress beneath. She moves forward to the noose. She kisses the noose and lays down the veil.*

END OF PLAY

Mona and Yadu'lláh Mahmúdni<u>zh</u>ád

Supplementary Materials

Glossary

'Abdu'l-Bahá: eldest son of Bahá'u'lláh (1844–1921), the exemplar of the Bahá'í teachings, and the leader of the Faith from 1892 to 1921. (ab-DOL-ba-HA)

Áyatu'lláh: a title referring to the most powerful priests within Shí'ih Islam. (AH-ya-TO-la)

Báb, The: the Prophet-Herald of the Bahá'í Faith (1819–1850). His revolutionary teachings resulted in brutal suppression by the Persian government and clergy. He was ultimately executed by firing squad. [See note 2] (bahb)

Bahá'í: a follower of the Bahá'í Faith, a religion that originated in Iran in the mid-19th Century. Bahá'ís make up the country's largest religious minority, and have often been the targets of persecution, most recently since the Islamic Revolution of the late 1970's. [See note 5] (Buh-HIGH)

Bahá'u'lláh: the Prophet-Founder of the Bahá'í Faith and its most important figure (1817–1892). His given name was Mírzá Husayn 'Alí; Bahá'u'lláh is a title that means "The Glory of God." He was from a noble Persian family, but was banished in 1852 at the height of persecutions against Bábís. A prisoner and exile for forty years, Bahá'u'lláh wrote voluminously, providing guidance and laying the foundations for what is now a worldwide religious community. (ba-HA-o-LA)

Chádor: a dark, full-length body veil, almost like a tent, to be worn by Iranian women in public. (cha-DOOR)

Imám: "leader" in Arabic. [See notes 16 and 37] (e-MAHM)

Iran: a country in southwest Asia, formerly known as Persia. (ir-RAHN)

Islam: the dominant religion of Iran and most of the near-Eastern countries. (es-LAHM)

Islamic call to prayer: One of the religious practices of Islam is for people to assemble several times a day to pray. The call to prayer is delivered by an individual, the *muezzin*, whose chanting signals the people to gather.

Kebáb: the Persian version of barbecue (also called *Shish Kabob*), consisting of prepared meat skewered onto sticks and cooked over an open flame. Traditionally, men make the kebáb. (ka-BAHB)

Mosque: an Islamic house of worship. (mosk)

Mullá: a title for a religious leader of the Shí'ih branch of Islam. (mol-LA)

Naw-Rúz: the Persian New Year, a festival which takes place for thirteen days starting on the first day of Spring. It's a time of joyfulness, generosity and hospitality. (no-ROOZ)

Persian: the predominant language and culture of Iran. *Persia* is the old name for Iran, and the people are alternately called Iranians or Persians. (PER-zhin)

Qur'án (also **Koran**): the holy book of Islam. It is written in the Arabic language and consists of writings ascribed to the Prophet Muhammad, 570-632 C.E.. (kor-AHN)

Sháh: the King of Iran. [see notes 10 and 11]

Shí'ih (also **Shiah, Shiite**): that branch of Islam predominant in Iran and some of its surrounding regions. (SHE-uh)

Shíráz: a major city in the south of Iran, famous for its roses and its poets, especially Hafez and Sa'di. (She-RAHZ)

Tadíg: the sweet and crunchy, slightly burnt portion at the bottom of the rice pot. It's often just rice, but can also be made from another starch such as potato or bread. (ta-DEEG)

Túmán: the Iranian paper currency. In 1982, this would be worth in the neighborhood of $100,000 to $200,000 U.S.. (TOO-mahn)

Notes on History and Sources

1. *"The* ROBED FIGURE *gestures right. A red dress is revealed . . ."* (I, i, 3)

    The portion of the dream about the three dresses is historical, while the rest is fictional. I heard Olya speak of this dream in October, 1994 in St. Petersburg, Florida as she was touring around the United States. I went home that night and typed up the basics:

    "Mona's favorite color was blue. Several months before she was imprisoned she had a dream. In Mona's dream, Bahá'u'lláh came to her. He said He had something to give her. He said that although He knew what her choice would be, she still had to choose from 3 alternatives. He went to the first box and pulled out a beautiful red dress of a very fine pattern and make. He dressed her in it and asked her if she liked it. She said it was beautiful but what did it mean? He told her that this was the garment of martyrdom. Would she like to wear this garment? Mona said, no, I don't wish to be a martyr. Bahá'u'lláh took the dress off her and opened the second box and retrieved another dress. This one was black, made of the same material and pattern and just as beautiful as the first. He dressed her as before and once again asked her if she liked it? Again she replied that it was beautiful but what did it mean? Bahá'u'lláh told her this was the garment of sadness and sorrow and would she like to wear this garment? Mona, once again, politely refused, saying she wasn't really interested in that. Bahá'u'lláh then pulled out a third dress similar to the others except blue and dressed her again, asking if she liked it. Mona again asked what it meant? Bahá'u'lláh replied that this was the garment of Service. Would she like to wear it? Mona was very happy with this one and told Bahá'u'lláh that she would like to wear this one very much."

    This is the version I heard in 1994. I think the spirit is correct if every detail is not. For example, I have since learned from my wife,

Azadeh, that Mona was not offered dresses but "shawls" (sh̲ál).
And yet I have a play constructed out of dresses and not shawls,
and for that I am thankful.

2. *It's a holy place."* (I, ii, 10)

   A couple of things here. The holy place referred to is known as the
   House of the Báb. This is the spot where on 22 May 1844, Siyyid 'Alí
   Muhammad, known as the Báb (or "the Gate"), declared His divine
   mission to His first follower, the event signaling the birth of a new
   religion, the Bahá'í Faith. Regarding the actual site, the street leading to it is more like an alley, and the style of the house doesn't per-
   mit one to look into the yard. Rather the outside has a high wall, and
   walking in, one enters the courtyard where the orange tree (planted
   by the Báb) would be located.

3. *"You can see where the guards tried to tear it down . . ."* (I, ii, 11)

   In its history and during the Revolution, the House of the Báb was
   several times vandalized. In the summer of 1979, officials confiscated the property, and demolition work was several times
   attempted, but then quickly suspended due to freak accidents, one
   of which is alluded to here. It was finally demolished in the dead of
   night in December of the same year. (See Olya's Story, pp. 20–27)

4. *"religious sect that all pious Muslims deem 'unclean' . . ."* (I, ii, 15)

   Unclean refers to a belief that certain people, animals or things are
   inherently impure and / or that association with them causes
   believers to enter a state of religious impurity (i.e., that without a
   ritualized purification, their prayers will be unacceptable to God.)

5. *"How can this be unless you are . . . a Baha'i?"* (I, ii, 16)

   Among the teachings of the Bahá'í Faith are that individuals should
   independently investigate the truth, that the clergy should be elim-
   inated, and that men and women are equal and should be granted
   equal opportunity. It furthermore claims the appearance of a Messenger of God after Muhammad, namely, Bahá'u'lláh (1817–1892).
   These teachings set it in direct opposition to the Shí'ih orthodoxy,
   which considers it an heretical sect. Despite this, the United Nations
   has acknowledged its independent status, and the Faith is well-
   established throughout the nations of the world with members representing every kind of racial and religious background. For more
   information: www.bahai.org

6. *"AQA HUSAYNI, a religious cleric (a "mulla"), enters"* (I, ii, 16)

Áqá is Persian for "Mister" and is a more common way to address a religious cleric than by the title, *Mullá*.

7. *"Everything was death and sex, death and sex!"* (I, iii, 22)

It is highly impolite and uncommon to speak of sex in a mixed social setting in Persian culture.

8. *"Those goons with the Revolutionary Guard . . ."* (I, iii, 23)

The *Revolutionary Guard* was an independent army raised up by the powerful Shí'ih clergy during the Islamic Revolution of the late 1970's. This Guard, separate from the regular army, enforced the will of the clergy, and was most directly responsible for the persecution of Bahá'ís.

9. *". . . this is an official request from the Baha'i community. I was asked, in my capacity as secretary, only to type it up."* (I, iii, 25)

Mona's father, Yadu'lláh Mahmudnizhad, served the Bahá'í community of Shíráz in several capacities as teacher, administrator and leader. Relevant here is his role as Secretary of the Local Spiritual Assembly. An L.S.A. is made up of 9 individuals elected annually who administer the affairs of the community. As secretary, his duties would be heavy and not that glorious. In this scene, the L.S.A. has apparently asked him communicate a request for Mona to be a teacher.

10. *"now the love of the Islamic Revolution is spreading!"* (I, iv, 30)

Iran's *Islamic Revolution* began in the late 1970's when the clergy and other discontented elements ousted the *Sháh*, the King of Iran, from power, and set up an "Islamic republic" run by the clergy.

11. *"now the Shah is dead!!"* (I, iv, 30)

The *Sháh*, Mohammed Reza Pahlaví, pressured from all sides to leave his country, finally did so in January 1979. He died of cancer an exile in 1980.

12. *"and Ayatu'llah Khomeini has returned . . ."* (I, iv, 30)

Áyatu'lláh Khomeini was the principal leader of the Islamic Revolution. In February 1979, he returned from a long exile to become the figurehead of the new government.

13. *"the Religious Magistrate of the Revolutionary Court."* (I, iv, 30)

As part of the Islamic Revolution, a new judicial system was set up that advanced the laws of the new theocratic state. The *Religious Magistrate* would then be a judge within these *Revolutionary Courts*.

14. *"Please welcome Ayatu'llah Qazá'í."* (I, iv, 30)

    Áyatu'llah Qazá'í was the powerful religious cleric who sentenced Mona and the other 9 women to be executed. He eventually was himself accused of some crime, arrested and tortured, losing an eye in the process.

15. *"Let us talk about 'Baha'i' . . ."* (I, iv, 31)

    The Bahá'ís have been denounced by the clergy in a number of ways, ranging from direct charges of apostasy, or abandonment of the true Faith, to more far-fetched claims of espionage on behalf of Israel and the West.

16. *"The Twelfth Imam has returned, Baha'i says."* (I, iv, 31)

    The *Twelve Imáms* were the great Shí'ih spiritual leaders descended from Muhammad. The Twelfth disappeared as a child, and Shí'ih prophecy forecasts his return.

17. *"I was asked to come and act as your teacher."* (I, iv, 31)

    Mona was a Bahá'í children's class teacher, following the model of her father, who worked with youth and young adults.

18. *"Ya Allah!"* (I, v, 34)

    Literally, "Yá Alláh!" means "O God!" but its use here is more like "Here I come!" Religious men will often use this exclamation to announce their presence before entering a house so that women inside can cover themselves.

19. *"Switch to* MR. ALIZADEH's *English class with* MONA, FARAH *and some other girls. All the girls wear thick clothing and head scarves."* (I, v, 35)

    The facts here: Mona was popular at school, she studied English, and she still attended school when most Bahá'í children had been expelled. As for the head scarves: before the Revolution of 1979, Iran had become quite westernized in its dress and entertainments. The Islamic Revolution gradually reintroduced more traditional practices, such as women covering up their hair in public.

20. *"Wwwwwwife! Speak it like an Arab!"* (I, v, 35)

    Persians pronounce their letter "Váv" as a "V", while the Arabs pronounce the same character as a "W." The people of Iran, while generally Muslim, are ethnically quite distinct from their Arab co-religionists. For one thing, the Persian language, while it has adopted the Arabic script and many Arabic words, is probably more closely related to Sanskrit or Latin.

21. *"is it not like Persian where you can just add the pronoun if you feel like it?"* (I, v, 36)

Here, Alizadeh is playing on a tendency in the Persian language to drop the pronoun. This can be done because the subject is implied in the verb ending. For example: The English phrase, "I went to the mountain" could be translated, "Man be kúh raftam" (literally, "I to mountain went") or "be kúh raftam" (literally, "to mountain went"). In the latter case, the verb ending "am" of "raftam" implies the first person singular, the "I."

22. *"Aram! Get out! Get out! You can't be here."* (I, v, 40)

Iran's public schools are segregated along gender lines. This was especially important so soon after the Revolution, as so much emphasis was placed on returning women to traditional roles and removing them from spheres frequented by non-related men and where their chastity might be endangered.

23. *"That girl is as much a spy for Israel . . ."* (I, v, 41)

[See note 15.]

24. *"The Site of the House of the Báb"* (I, vi, 45)

According to Olya, Mona did make a pilgrimage to the ruins of the House of the Báb. This and the Bahá'í response to persecution appeared to have a profound effect on her. [See note 3.]

25. *"Mama. I don't wish to take off my shoes . . ."* (I, vii, 49)

Again, according to Olya, this was her response upon returning from the site.

26. *"Bismulláh'u'l-rahmán-i-rahím . . ."* (I, vii, 55)

This is the opening verse of the Qur'án, which translates, "In the name of God, the Merciful, the Compassionate."

27. *"Come on, come on. You'll just be next door. [They exit with* MONA *. . ."* (I, vii, 63)

There is no indication that Mona left the apartment. This is intended to heighten dramatic effect and clarify her choice-making.

28. *"We are from the Revolutionary Court of Shiraz. We have a warrant to enter your house from the Public Prosecutor."* (I, vii, 63)

This line and several others in this arrest scene are either para-phrased or taken verbatim from Olya's Story, p. 129–130.

29. *"One is recently married . . ."* (I, vii, 64)

This refers to Mona's older sister, Taránih. She was married and out of the house at the time of the arrest. Reference to her is also made in Act II, Scene 1.

30. *"Do you know who this is? / That is Mr. Bakhtavar."* (I, vii, 65)

Again, taken from the actual account. Mr. Bakhtávar was a promi-nent Iranian Bahá'í who had already been executed at this point.

31. *"Dear Farah, I'm even wondering if you'll get this . . ."* (II, i, 71)

Mona surprisingly managed to send out a couple of letters while in prison. This and several other aspects of this fictional letter are fac-tual. Likewise, many of the details in this scene are gleaned from descriptions in Olya's account.

32. *"he wouldn't have banned them if they didn't work."* (II, i, 73)

When Bahá'ís first began to be brought to prison, they would chant prayers together. The other prisoners and the guards were moved by them, so the Religious Magistrate banned the Bahá'ís from praying.

33. *"It's a real release. Whether they let you go is another matter . . ."* (II, i, 74)

Orders for Mona's release were issued at least twice. On one occa-sion, as dramatized here, her mother came with the required 500,000 Túmán as security bond and was told the security bond was for herself. In reality, the reversal of fortune was worse than indi-cated here, for the mother had to turn herself in within 24 hours, and as a result, she spent 5 months in prison. She was released only five days before Mona was executed.

34. *"The Iranian people are kept in poverty while the oil-rich bastard traitors and their English friends make millions!"* (II, i, 79)

Because of its rich oil resources, Iran became very important to the West in the 20th Century. The countries of the West, especially England, and later the U.S., took a special interest in Iran.

35. *"OOOOOOOOHHHHHH!!! Ya Baha'u-l'abha!!"* (II, i, 82)

Yá Bahá'u-l'abhá, or "O Glory of the Most Glorious," is an invoca-tion, or a calling out to God. It is used by Baha'is in times of great joyfulness or other emotional extremity.

36. *"O God, I want my child. I want Mona from you . . . my little bird is trapped in a cage."* (II, i, 82)

From Mona's mother's account, Olya's Story, p. 134.

37. *"Did Imam Husayn do well in dying for his faith?"* (II, ii, 89)

Imám Husayn was the third Imam of Shí'ih Islam, and generally considered the most tragic of its martyrs. He, his family and a band of his followers were slaughtered by a rival Muslim faction. Each year on the anniversary of his martyrdom, a great mourning with elaborate processions is raised throughout Iran.

38. *"And yet 'Abdu'l-Baha said you could lie to a dying man . . ."* (II, ii, 92)

"There is no worse characteristic than this [lying]; it is the foundation of all evils. Notwithstanding all this, if a doctor consoles a sick man by saying, 'Thank God you are better, and there is hope of your recovery,' though these words are contrary to the truth, yet they may become the consolation of the patient and the turning point of the illness. This is not blameworthy."

— 'Abdu'l-Bahá, Some Answered Questions, pp. 215–216

39. *"Bahá'u'lláh: 'The most burning fire is to question the signs of God . . ."* (II, ii, 93)

"The most burning fire is to question the signs of God, to dispute idly that which He hath revealed, to deny Him and carry one's self proudly before Him."

— Bahá'u'lláh, Tablets of Bahá'u'lláh, p. 156

40. *"Prisoners Visitation Room . . ."* (II, iv, 101)

This meeting conflates at least three different meetings: one of several meetings in which Mona's mother came to visit Mona in prison (Olya's Story, pp. 134-135), a discussion between Mona and her mother when they were both in prison (pp. 219–221), and a brief meeting the three had together in prison before the father's execution (pp. 138-139). Several of the lines in this scene are paraphrased or quoted from the account.

41. *"Your parents have deceived and misled you . . . They have forced you to imitate them in following the Baha'i religion."* (II, iv, 108)

These lines and several that follow thereafter are paraphrases or quotes from Mona's final trial. (Olya's Story, pp. 132–133)

42. *"Now if by Islam you mean the hatred and bloodshed going on in this country, now that is the reason I'm a Baha'i!"* (II, iv, 109)

This line is a paraphrase of something Mona said to the Religious Magistrate and is recorded in an extract written by Olya, and published in Unrestrained as the Wind (p. 53).

43. *"The doors open and the* FATHER *is wheeled in on a gurney, seated upright.* MONA *goes to embrace him, then jumps back . . ."* (II, iv, 110)

    This event did not actually occur.

44. *"We must obey the Qur'an. Accept Islam or face execution / I kiss the order of execution."* (II, iv, 112)

    Excerpted from Olya's Story, p. 133.

45. *"What do you want? / Perseverance. / What do you want from me? . . ."* (II, iv, 112)

    This is a dream Mona had in prison. The questioner was 'Abdu'l-Bahá.

46. *"Last. I want to be last . . . I want to pray for the others."* (II, iv, 113)

    According to a witness' testimony, Mona was indeed last of the ten. (Olya's Story, p. 225)

47. *"She kisses the noose and lays down the veil."* (II, iv, 113)

    I don't know of any documentation of this, but she had said to her mother that she would first kiss the hand of her executioner, and then kiss the rope she was to be hanged with. (Olya's Story, p. 220)

Notes on Readings

Readings are good low-budget ways to experience plays. If you would like to do a reading (i.e., have a group read the play out loud), there are a couple of things to consider:

First, you will want to decide if you want a formal or informal reading. In a formal reading, the room is divided between readers and audience, the way a theatre generally is. In the stage area, there is a chair for each reader. (In this play, you may want 9 readers all together: 8 for character roles, and 1 for stage directions.) Each of the readers has a script, while the audience generally does not. In other ways, the formal reading follows the basic rules of theatre-going. Some preparation or rehearsal is important. For most occasions, one or two group "read-throughs" before the presentation will be sufficient. Taken further, "staged readings" incorporate some blocking (or stage movement), more developed scene work, and even simple props. In a less formal reading, such as one might want in a classroom or study circle, everyone will probably have access to a script, and, depending on the size of the group, the character roles can either be spread out more or heaped up higher.

Second, this play takes place in Iran, and the readers should be prepared for the Persian and Arabic words they will encounter. (See *Persian Pronunciation Guide*, p. 127) A single foreign word can cause a hiccup in a reading, but a string of them can induce cardiac arrest. "Mahmud-nizhad," for example, is a mouthful and is said dozens of times throughout the play. I recommend that readers learn this name before presenting the play. If the opening dream sequence is difficult to the point of frustration, then the English translations can be read instead.

Persian Pronunciation Guide

Observing just a few rules, a Persian accent can be fairly well approximated:

1. Vowel sounds
   a. When vowels have accents*
      á like a in "father" or o in "dog"
      í like ee in "cheese"
      ú like oo in "shoot"
   b. When vowels have no accents
      a like a in "cat"
      e or i like e in "get"
      o or u like o in "go"
2. Consonant sounds
   a. Most consonant sounds are similar to English.
   b. <u>Kh</u>, <u>Gh</u>, and Q are guttural sounds, unfamiliar to English speakers. Appropriately, "<u>kh</u>" is midway between a "k" and a "h" and "<u>gh</u>" (and "q") is midway between a "g" and a "h." These are difficult sounds for many, so an easy compromise is pronouncing "<u>kh</u>" as "k," and "<u>gh</u>" (and "q") as "g."
3. Stress
   a. Give all syllables more or less equal stress.
   b. Fight the English tendency to speak in, iambs or any other stressed / unstressed combination.

---

* For character names, see the character list (pp. xv–xvwi) for proper transliteration and approximated pronunciations. For Persian and Arabic terms used in the text without proper accents, see the Glossary.

Notes from the First Production

There are some challenges inherent in this script. The following notes are offered in a spirit of collaboration, the kind of things that might be broached over a cup of coffee before the first rehearsal.

Casting

Minimum cast requirements are 4 female and 4 male. This minimum takes a little bit of fudging with the script, but can basically be achieved by having one female play Farah, Zahra, and Guard (in I, vii), another female playing Mrs. Khudayar, School Secretary, and Head Prisoner, and then the Mother doubling as Girl (in I, v). The dream sequence (I, i) requires ensemble work, and 2 silent hooded figures are also needed (II, iv). Optional non-speaking roles are classmates (I, v), mourners (I, vi), religious men (I, vi), extra guards (I, vii; II, i; & II, iv), and extra prisoners (II, i).

The challenge of a good character

Perhaps the most significant lesson that I learned about how to perform this play came on opening night. By most accounts, opening night was a bad night. You know how it goes: the people in the audience that you know avoid talking to you or looking you in the eye. Apart from my own embarrassment, I was wondering what kind of constructive feedback I could give to the actors. As it worked out, most of us ended up going out for pizza and laughing about the screw-ups and botched lines.

One really positive moment from that night's performance that we discussed was the way Kehry Lane (who was portraying the Father) delivered the *"These men, these men, I love these brothers like my own sons . . ."* line at the end of Act I. It's a wonderful aria of sorts that is almost word-for-word from the historical account. And on this night, Kehry was clearly moved and present in delivering the line. The urgency shook his body. He seemed to embody both the telescoping fear that comes from an awareness of great danger, and the indomitable courage to do the right thing in the face of that fear. And the words soared phoenix-like from the ashen platitude of the page.

As discussed in the introduction, saints can be tricky material for drama. We must remember their humanity. After all, did their blood not race when the guards entered the apartment? Did their voices not quaver when answering their interrogators? Did their conscience not face down the diametrical opposition of every physical fibre in the body? The body wills to live, but the soul will not sacrifice truth — its reality! — for an ephemeral concern. The disciplined rider drives the frighted charger into the line of fire because that's where the glory is. Even if the martyrs and saints have transcended fear, consider the electricity, the rarefied atmosphere, surrounding them in their moments of trial. Consider the following statement from Bahá'u'lláh:

> By My life, O friend, wert thou to taste of these fruits [of communion with God] . . . yearning would seize the reins of patience and reserve from out thy hand, and *make thy soul to shake with the flashing light*, and draw thee from the earthly homeland to the first, heavenly abode in the Center of Realities.[1]

Though we may not assume such a profound, dare I say, such a Dionysian, transformation will overtake our beloved actors, yet in this image of the clashing of fear and courage, we find a tool to assist us. To paraphrase 'Abdu'l-Bahá: from the clash of differing passions, the shining spark of truth comes forth.[2]

Persian Pronunciation

The *Persian Pronunciation Guide* (p. 127) may be helpful if the cast is unfamiliar with the language. This is especially meant for the opening sequence of Persian phrases. Throughout the rest of the play, it seems to me that anglicizing the pronunciations will make the occasional foreign term less of a pothole in the path. The pronunciations included in the

---

1 The Seven Valleys and The Four Valleys, pp. 3-4 (emphasis added)
2 Cf. 'Abdu'l-Bahá, Selections from the Writings of 'Abdu'l-Bahá, p. 93.

Glossary should help with this. The most important thing for me when directing a cast of non-Persians was to make the names and phrases seem effortless and consistent, even if they were technically mispronounced. This was so that the action of the play would not be interrupted unnecessarily with a sound of foreignness.

Staging challenges

Act I, Scene 2 finds Mona and Farah walking through the streets of Shiraz and then coming to the House of the Báb. In the first production, we made the aisle ways of the theatre the street on which Mona and Farah are walking. They re-entered the stage area on "This is it" and a lighting change indicated the arrival at the entrance to the House. The center aisle then became the entrance way to the house, and the audience became the holy place.

In Act II, Scene 4, the scene begins in the prison's visitation area, and the voices of Mona and the Father can be heard, but the Mother's cannot. We did not actually use a piece of glass to separate them, but we did use lighting to differentiate one side of the glass from the other. The Mother's silence then was "acted" rather than being muted by a material barrier. A further question is how to place the two on stage so that we're not looking at Mona's back throughout. We decided instead to initially put the Mother really far downstage and have Mona face the audience. Then when the Father entered, the Mother moved to another "booth," this time upstage of Mona and the Father. In any case, it's a challenge to be aware of, an opportunity for invention. I resisted "fixing" this, deciding that the silence of the Mother, her placement behind an impermeable barrier separated from daughter and husband, is too key an image to dispense with.

Finally, in the first production, we didn't use a noose. She simply walked forward, and laid her chador atop the nine other dresses. I don't think there was any question what was happening.

Lighting and the Aram / Young Man / Magistrate character

This is a story that not only takes place in some locations in this world, but also punctures the physical barrier seeking to access the next world, that "world of lights." Lighting is one way I hoped to communicate this. We had about 70 lighting cues in an otherwise fairly bare-bones production. Not every production of this play has to have this many (or this few), but there are a couple of areas that deserve mentioning:

A basic motif of the play is the dream of the three dresses and the appearance of the Young Man in it. The character that maneuvers among the personae of Aram, the Religious Magistrate and the Young Man may need "technical" assistance in clarifying the transformations from one character to the next. One way to think of this persona shift is this: Aram is very much of this world, the Young Man is very much of the next world, the Religious Magistrate stands at the threshold between the two (as the one who sentences Mona to death), but the "character" lives in the whole spectrum. So, very loosely speaking, the Young Man appears in a spirit / dream-like light, Aram appears in normal light, and the Religious Magistrate lurks in a shadowy place between the two.

Lighting and Mona's world

Another related element that we discovered in the process was how lighting can either open or confine Mona's world. The world of the play is very open at the beginning of the play. Mona and Farah walk through the audience as if it were the streets of a city. By the second act, Mona is confined to the stage area even as she is confined in prison. By the end, as she is being interrogated, the world of the play seems to be very small indeed, so small that it is placed by the Magistrate at the threshold of her nostrils: *"You feel that hot, moist breath surging in and out of your nostrils . . . I can take that away too."* And yet, the play does not end there. While we know her breath is extinguished at the end of the play, no body litters the stage. Rather the play enters the next world with Mona and the other women, and we perceive, as they do, how these bodies we call our "selves" may be seen only as dresses, as veils disguising truth. As the play enters that world, the space must open up again and, if possible, wider than before.

Sound

The sound actually called for in the script is minimal: a P.A. set-up for the "Intercom" voices and a handful of sound-effects (a kettle, a school bell, some loud whip-like cracks). Except for music and chanting, the only other cue we added was a bass hum sound-effect at the appearance of the Religious Magistrate (I, iv) and during the "perseverance" exchange near the end (II, iv). As for the music, it seemed to be quite valuable in establishing place and mood, especially with such minimal design elements. If you're having a hard time finding Iranian music, contact the Publisher.

Works Cited

'Abdu'l-Bahá, <u>Selections from the Writings of 'Abdu'l-Bahá</u>. (trans. by Marzieh Gail and committee). Wilmette, IL: Bahá'í Publishing Trust, 1997.

'Abdu'l-Bahá, <u>Some Answered Questions</u>. (trans. by Laura Clifford-Barney). Wilmette, IL: Bahá'í Publishing Trust, 1930.

Bahá'í National Youth Committee, <u>Unrestrained as the Wind.</u> Wilmette, IL: Bahá'í Publishing Trust: 1985.

Bahá'u'lláh, <u>The Seven Valleys and the Four Valleys</u>. (trans. by Marzieh Gail). Wilmette, IL: Bahá'í Publishing Trust, 1952.

Bahá'u'lláh, <u>Tablets of Bahá'u'lláh, revealed after the Kitab-i-Aqdas</u>. (trans. by Habib Taherzadeh and committee). Wilmette, IL: Bahá'í Publishing Trust, 1988.

Roohizadegan, Olya, <u>Olya's Story</u>. Oxford: Oneworld Publications, 1993.

Rumi, Jalálu'd-Dín, <u>Like This: more poems of Rumi.</u> (audiobook, trans. and read by Coleman Barks). Berkeley, CA: Audio Literature, 1989.

5TH EPOCH PRESS

To view our other titles and
to order more copies of

A Dress for Mona

visit our website at

www.discoverwriting.com

Phone: 1-800-613-8055 • Fax: 1-802-897-2084

Or mail in the form below with your check, credit card or purchase order.

METHOD OF PAYMENT: ☐ Check or money order enclosed ☐ Purchase order attached P.O.#_____

☐ Mastercard ☐ Visa ☐ Discover Card

Signature_____

Credit Card#_____Exp.Date_____

PLEASE PRINT

NAME _____ HOME PHONE _____

HOME ADDRESS_____

CITY_____ STATE _____ ZIP CODE _____

TITLE	PRICE	QTY	AMOUNT
A DRESS FOR MONA	$10.00		
Shipping & Handling $3.95 plus $1 for ea. additional item			
VT Residents add 5%			
Make check payable to: DWC, P.O. Box 264, Shoreham, VT 05770	**TOTAL**		